International Passenger Locomotives

Since 1985

ANDY FLOWERS

WORLD RAILWAYS SERIES, VOLUME 1

Title page image: The E.656 is a 3,000V DC Bo-Bo-Bo design and 461 were built between 1975 and 1989 by Officine Casaralta, Officine Reggiane, SOFER, TIBB componentistica Ercole Marelli, Ansaldo, Asgen and Italtrafo. With a one-hour rating of 6,440hp and a top speed of 93mph, the type, nicknamed 'Cairmano' ('Caiman', a crocodile-like reptile), was used on a wide range of freight traffic and passenger work. Some E.656s, the last of a long line of Italian articulated locos, were re-geared to exclusively undertake freight work, becoming Class E655. E656 603 stands at Milan Central after arrival on a regional service on 26 February 2011.

Published by Key Books
An imprint of Key Publishing Ltd
PO Box 100
Stamford
Lincs PE19 1XQ

www.keypublishing.com

The right of Andy Flowers to be identified as the author
of this book has been asserted in accordance with the
Copyright, Designs and Patents Act 1988 Sections 77 and 78.

Copyright © Andy Flowers, 2020

ISBN 978 1 913295 92 9

20 21 22 23 24   10 9 8 7 6 5 4 3 2 1

Typeset by SJmagic DESIGN SERVICES, India.

Contents

Introduction

As the number of locomotive-hauled passenger trains in the UK began to decline in the 1980s, many haulage enthusiasts, particularly those keen to travel behind as many different locomotives as possible, began to spread their wings and travel abroad in search of new locomotives. While some 'bashers', particularly fans of the German V200 'Warships' (similar to the popular Western Region BR diesel hydraulics), used a similar pattern to those following particular classes of locomotive in Britain, most British enthusiasts took the opportunity to run amok in a frenzy of red pen underlining of new locomotives in their haulage books. This pattern of activity remains to this day but with horizons spread even further afield, to countries such as the USA and even many that are seldom visited by most members of the British public.

As bashers began to take more interest in foreign railways their travels echoed in many ways the expansion of colonisation, though with the nearby European countries explored first, particularly France, the Netherlands, Germany and Belgium. The availability of decent beer in Germany and Belgium was also a big draw for many rail enthusiasts and meant a higher number of visitors.

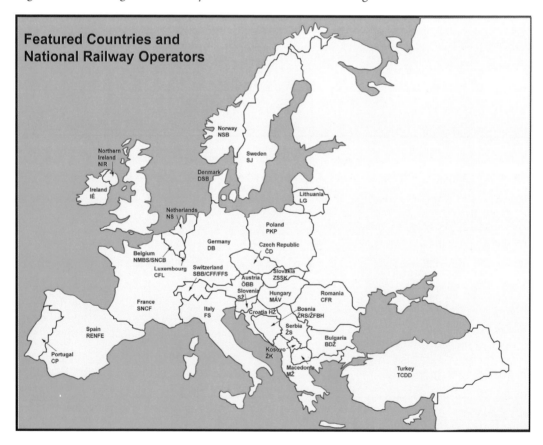

Featured Countries and National Railway Operators

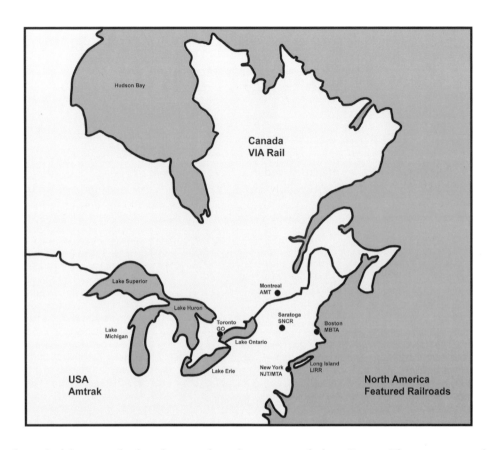

By the end of the 1980s, bashers began to branch out, particularly to Eastern Bloc countries such as East Germany, Poland and Czechoslovakia. Poland and East Germany in particular saw steam still in service until a late date and Czechoslovakia had the joint attractions of cheap and good-quality beer and loud diesel locomotives like the Class 751 'Zamračená', which resembled the BR Class 37s in terms of sound output. Portugal also became a popular destination with the Class 1400s (a Class 20 derivative) and 1800s (similar to the BR Class 50s).

In more recent years, bashing has expanded to countries such as India, Israel, the USA and Thailand with enthusiasts attracted by the number of locomotive-hauled trains still available.

In terms of classifying the various types of locomotives powering the world's railway networks it is perhaps easier to break down the different types by the manufacturing company, rather than by country or operator (see the table on pages 91–96). Since the end of the Second World War, though many countries (including, until recently, the UK) have their own indigenous locomotive-manufacturing industry, a few countries, particularly the USA, Germany and France, have dominated the market with companies like EMD, Alstom and Siemens gaining an ever-increasing market share, selling locomotives off the shelf ready to run or granting licences for construction of their own designs in purchasing countries.

Moving to the 2020s, locomotive haulage of passenger trains is still in decline around the world, though the number of EMUs being introduced has stabilised. The possibilities of hearing loud diesel locomotives hauling open-air stock are rapidly diminishing, though in a pattern similar to that seen in the UK, a few areas are bucking the trend. In particular, Portugal is seeing a reintroduction of open-air Schindler stock and the highly popular 1400s. Bashing worldwide is far from dead.

Chapter 1

Austria

The national operator is *Österreichische Bundesbahnen* (ÖBB).

Originally built as the DR Class E94 and known in Germany as the Class 194 (DB) or 254 (DR), the ÖBB Class 1020 was a heavy freight electric locomotive built by AEG, BBC, Henschel, Krauss-Maffei and Krupp between 1940 and 1956. In total, 231 of the locos were built, operating on 15kV 16⅔Hz AC with a top speed of 62mph and an output of 4,429hp. After the war, 42 of the locos were allocated to the Austrian railway with a further three examples ordered in 1952. The last Austrian locos were withdrawn in 1995. 'Crocodile' 1020 034 is attached to the rear of EC168, the 11.00 Graz–Zurich, at Landeck.

The Class 1046s were rebuilt from Class 4061 luggage motor cars (renumbered in 1976) and were dual-voltage locos used on services into the Czech Republic and Hungary. The 13 locos had a top speed of 87mph and a relatively low output of 2,000hp. They were introduced in 1956 and outshopped in traditional green livery. However, the type was reliveried into standard ÖBB red colours before the fleet was withdrawn in 2003, replaced from their Vienna commuter duties, together with the Class 1042s, by new Class 1116 'Taurus' locos. Here, 1046 001 is seen at Sigmundsherberg on a regional service to Wien Franz Josef in 1992.

ÖBB ordered 50 Centre Cab Class 1063s from Siemens, delivered between 1983 and 1991, for heavy shunting duties. With a top speed of 62mph and an output of 2,700hp they also proved useful on secondary passenger duties. 1063 019 stands at Pregarten on 3 September 1992 on train D475, the 06.21 Prague hlavní nádraží to Linz. Ten examples of the larger and heavier, but physically similar, Class 1064s were also produced, mostly for heavy yard shunting. The 1163s currently in use with ÖBB, mostly for shunting duties, are an updated version of the 1063s.

The EuroSprinter, 'Taurus' or ES64, family of electric locomotives, suitable for a wide range of duties, were built by Siemens for continental European railways. The ES64 designation comes from the impressive 6,400kW rating at the rail (8,600hp). Geared for 87 or 140mph running, the type has been sold to a wide range of railways including DB, ÖBB, MÁV, SŽ and PKP. The 'Taurus' family has proven popular with enthusiasts due to their good looks and impressive performance, particularly on the 140mph RailJet services. 1216 025 holds the world speed record for a conventional locomotive, having reached 222mph near Nurnberg in 2006. Production of the ES64s has been discontinued by Siemens as newer locomotives are now available in the Vectron series. On 16 February 2010, ÖBB 'Taurus' 1216 238 stands at Prague hlavní nádraží.

The Mariazellbahn, from St. Pölten to Mariazell, is a 760mm narrow-gauge Austrian branch line, electrified at 6.5kV with a frequency of 25Hz. Electric locos were introduced when electrification began in 1911, with the 16E series locomotives (now Class 1099) being brought in between 1911 and 1914 and rebuilt in the 1960s with their current body design. The 16 examples of the Class 1099 electric locos were replaced by Stadler EMUs between 2012 and 2014, though some examples have been retained for special workings. Here, 1099 003 is seen at Ober Grafendorf on train 6830, the 11.30 St. Pölten–Mariazell on 18 February 1992.

Introduced in 1958, the 15 examples of the 760mm-gauge diesel hydraulic Class 2095s were built by Simmering-Graz-Pauker between 1958 and 1962 and were widely used on ÖBB's narrow-gauge lines. With a maximum speed of 37mph and a power output of 600hp, they were used on both freight and passenger duties. Here, 2095 015 *Mank* is seen at Ober Grafendorf on 18 February 1992 on a local service on the Mariazellbahn. The railway has retained some Class 2095s for special workings.

Chapter 2

Belgium

The national operators are:

Dutch – **Nationale Maatschappij der Belgische Spoorwegen (NMBS).**
French – **Société Nationale des Chemins de fer Belges (SNCB).**

SNCB's Class 16s (originally Class 160s) were used almost exclusively for cross-border passenger traffic, operating on four different voltages. Six of the type were built in 1966 by BN/ACEC with an output of 3,728hp and a top speed of 100mph. They were replaced on these duties by Thalys (TGV style) EMUs in the noughties and saw out their days on some peak-hours Brussels commuter services before being withdrawn in 2007 with two examples preserved. In January 1990, 1605 waits at Ostend with a service to Cologne. The train was clearly the last booked working for the guard and was suitably adorned with a headboard. The reason for the baking foil over the buffers was less clear.

Alsthom produced six of the multi-voltage Class 18s between 1973 and 1974 for use on international services for SNCB, including Ostend to Cologne and Paris/Brussels to Liège. Not to be confused with the modern Class 18s produced by Siemens for SNCB, the French locos, based on the SNCF CC 40100 locos, had an output of 5,790hp and a top speed of 112mph. The fleet was withdrawn by the end of 1999 with 1805 preserved. Multi-voltage SNCB electric loco 1801 arrives at Aachen in 1991 with a service from Ostend to Cologne.

Built by BN and ACEC between 1964 and 1971, the 35-strong fleet of Class 26s were 3,000V DC B-B electric locos, featuring monomotor bogies, with a one-hour rating of 3,500hp and a top speed of 62 or 83mph (the gear ratio could be chosen for freight or passenger work). The class shared many features with the SNCF's Class BB 9400s. Dedicated largely to freight traffic for much of their career, near the end of their working lives the class were allocated to Louvain-la-Neuve-Université to Binche regional services, working the trains top and tail. The class was withdrawn at the end of 2011. Here, on 15 April 2011, 2607 arrives at Binche with 2624 on the rear ready to work the return service.

The NMBS/SNCB Type 29 2-8-0s were supplied to Belgium by Canada and the USA in 1945 and 1946 following the Second World War, as part of the Marshall Plan, to assist the rebuilding effort. The fleet of 300 was built to one design by three separate manufacturers – the Montreal Locomotive Works (160 locos), the American Locomotive Company (80 locos) and the Canadian Locomotive Company (60 locos). 29.013 was preserved for display at Train World, the Belgian national railway museum at Schaarbeek railway station in Brussels. The Type 29 was rated at 2,000hp with a nominal top speed of 50mph and a similar design was supplied to China as the KD7, also for freight duties. On Saturday 19 May 2012, 'Baldwin' 29013 waits at Couvin during a photo stop on a Mercia Trains Charter from Brussels to Mariembourg and Treignes (the Chemin de Fer des Trois Valées preserved line). Class 77 7757 was provided on the rear for shunt release and short sections of the trip.

The NMBS/SNCB Class 51s were an early Co-Co diesel-electric design produced by Cockerill between 1961 and 1963. Ninety-three locos were built with a top speed of 75mph and an output of 1,950hp. SNCB used the class more generally on heavy freight traffic in pairs before withdrawal in 2003. Six members of the class were preserved after the fleet was withdrawn and two examples were sold on to private operators in Sicily. 5111 enters Gent-Sint-Pieters to work a service to Antwerp on 15 June 2001.

The Belgian Class 52 Nohabs were used mostly on freight services between Namur and Athus with one regular passenger turn from Bertrix to Namur. Complaints about draughts from the crews led to new cabs being fitted, which substantially altered the loco's appearance when compared to the Nohabs in use throughout the rest of Europe. SNCB Nohabs with their boilers removed were reclassified as Class 53s. Here, 5211 stands at Dinant on 19 September 1992 on L7610, the 10.23 service to Bertrix. The Nohab fleet was withdrawn in Belgium in 2009.

Built in 1961 and 1962 under licence by La Brugeoise et Nivelles, rather than AFB, the 42 NMBS/SNCB Co-Co Class 55s are powered by a heavily silenced GM 16-567C power unit generating 1,934hp and have a top speed of 75mph. Introduced originally as Class 205s as a development of the Nohabs with the newer cab style, they were Belgium's standard diesel locomotive for passenger work. They were also produced for Luxembourg (Class 1800s) as a follow-on order. Around 20 of the fleet are still active for freight and civil engineering duties, with six fitted for the haulage of TGVs on the high-speed line to Paris. The class no longer has any booked passenger workings though they may appear at the Chemin de Fer du Bocq galas held annually. Here, 5510 stands at Luxembourg on a train for Liège in 1991.

The Class 62 became NMBS/SNCB's standard diesel locomotive with 136 being built by BN/ACEC between 1961 and 1966. With a 1,400hp GM 12-567C power unit, push-pull facilities and a top speed of 75mph, the locos worked a large proportion of Belgian diesel loco-hauled passenger duties up until their replacement by units in the noughties. Many of the locos remain in service with Infrabel (the infrastructure maintenance wing of the state railway system). Here, 6304 stands at Gent-Sint-Pieters on the 16.02 to Ronse on 15 June 2001.

Chapter 3

Bosnia

Two companies operate services in the ethnically divided country following the Dayton Agreement:

Republika Srpska Railways (ŽRS), which operates in Republika Srpska.
Railways of the Federation of Bosnia and Herzegovina (ŽFBH), which operates in the Federation of Bosnia and Herzegovina.

ŽFBH 441 911 waits at Sarajevo on 18 August 2012 on the daily service to Mostar. Designed by ASEA, the ex-JŽ Class 441s have a top speed of 62, 75, 87 or 99mph, dependent on gearing, and a power output of up to 6,800hp. Sarajevo station is equipped more than adequately for the mere handful of trains it receives every day.

The JŽ Class 441 was a Swedish ASEA-designed electric locomotive built for Yugoslav Railways by a group of companies comprising 50 Hz Traction Union (ASEA, SAAS Sécheron, SGP/Simmering-Graz-Pauker) (1968–70), Končar Group, TŽV Janko Gredelj, Đuro Đaković, MIN Niš (1970–87) and UCM Reşiţa. The locomotives are now used by Hrvatske željeznice (HŽ reclassified them as 1141), Željeznice Federacije Bosne i Hercegovine, Željeznice Republike Srpske/Жељезнице Републике Српске (the Serbian-led railway authority in Bosnia and Herzegovina), Serbian Railways, Rail transport of TPP Nikola Tesla (a power plant near Belgrade), Makedonski Železnici, Turkish State Railways and Romanian Railways-CFR. On 17 August 2012, ŽRS Class 441 441 114 waits at Doboj on the international Budapest to Sarajevo service.

Chapter 4

Bulgaria

The national operator is (in Bulgarian) **Български държавни железници, Balgarski darzhavni zheleznitsi;** abbreviated as **БДЖ, BDZ** or **BDŽ.**

The BDŽ, a Škoda-built electric locomotive, is essentially an upgraded version of the Class 43 with an electrodynamic brake. Designated as type 68 E by the manufacturer, and with 149 examples delivered in the mid-1970s, it became the standard electric motive power on Bulgarian railways. The Class 45s are differentiated by a lower top speed (68 as opposed to 81mph). The passenger sector kept most of the class after sectorisation in 2012 with only 12 going to the cargo division. On 21 February 2013, 44 078 stands at Sofia Central with the overnight sleeper service to Belgrade.

Ten of the 75 Class (Bosnian) 760mm-gauge diesel hydraulics were built in 1966 by Henschel and Sohn of Kassel, Germany, and feature steam-heating boilers, a Maybach Mb 820 power unit giving, 1,100hp and a top speed of 43mph. Similar locos were exported to Togo, Thailand and Spain. Three members of the fleet remain in service. They are operated by BDŽ and used on the 77.5-mile-long Septemvri to Dobrinishte branch, the 'Rhodope' line. Septemvri is the junction station on the main line from Sofia to Plovdiv. This is the only operating public narrow-gauge line still operating in Bulgaria. On 20 February 2013, 75 008 stands at Velingrad (Велинград) on a train to Dobrinishte.

The Bulgarian Class 07 'Ludmilla' is a Russian design, identical to the DB/DR Class 130/131, supplied by Voroshilovgrad Locomotive Works of Ukraine when it was part of the USSR, with 2,950 installed horsepower, a top speed of 62mph and no installed train heating. Ninety were imported from 1971 for BDŽ use with an additional two transferred later from ČSD. They are Bulgaria's premier diesel for heavy freight and passenger use. The five Class 07.1s are a rebuild with ETH capability installed. On 19 February 2013, 07126 stands at Plovdiv on the 18.20 working to Pesthera.

Chapter 5

Canada

Nationwide passenger services are provided by the federal crown corporation **VIA Rail**.

AMT (Agence Métropolitaine de Transport) of Montreal (now renamed Exo) ordered 20 dual-mode Bo-Bo locomotives from Bombardier in 2008 to replace the remaining GP9s and F40PHRs in use on commuter traffic on the Vaudreuil-Hudson, Saint-Jérôme, Mont-Saint-Hilaire and Mascouche lines into Montreal Central Station. The ALP-45DP is a development of the ALP-46A and TRAXX locos using two 12-cylinder Caterpillar 3512C HD power units rated at 2,100hp each with around 6,000hp available on electric mode. Numbered 1350 to 1369, the first of the locos was delivered via Newark in 2011 after assembly in Wrocław. Though the design (also in use with New Jersey Transit) is capable of 125mph electric running and 100mph on diesel, on AMT they are restricted to 80 and 60mph respectively. On 27 June 2014, 1368 arrives at Montreal Ouest on a train from Hudson to Montreal Lucien L'Aller on the Ligne Vaudreuil-Hudson.

The F59PH was the first member of the F59 family of locos. Produced by EMD between 1988 and 1994, 73 of the locos were supplied to GO transit of Toronto and Metrolink of Los Angeles. Many of the GO locomotives were later sold to other commuter operators, including ten to AMT of Montreal (now Exo) for use on the Candiac, Vaudreuil-Hudson and Mont-Saint-Hilaire lines. With a 3,000hp EMD 12-710G3A power unit and full-width cab, the locos have a top speed of 90mph. Here, 1345 leaves Montreal Ouest on 27 June 2014 on a train from Montreal Lucien L'Aller to Candiac on the Ligne Candiac.

The F59PHI is an uprated streamlined version of the F59PH, designed for Amtrak's Californian intercity service, and production began in 1994. Seventy-four examples of the F59PHI were built and ordered by Amtrak, MetroLink and commuter bodies in Seattle, Vancouver, North Carolina and Montreal. EMD, as well as GE, was drafted in to design replacements for its successful F40 design. GO (Government of Ontario) Transit ordered 16 F59PHs, which were delivered in 1988 and 1989 and rated at 3,000hp. Other buyers included MetroLink in Los Angeles and 79 F59PHIs were built between 1988 and 1994. It is distinguished from the F59PH by its streamlined cab. Eighty-three F59PHIs were built between 1994 and 2001, mostly for commuter operators, including AMT, as was the case with 1323, shown here on 27 June 2014 at Montreal Lucien L'Aller on a train to Hudson on the Ligne Vaudreuil-Hudson. Other major operators include Metra (of Chicago), Metrolink (California) and Sound Transit (Seattle). With a 3,200hp EMD 12-710G3C-EC power unit they are rated at 110mph though generally operated at lower speeds due to stock and track constraints.

The MPXpress family is a design of modern diesel-electrics for commuter traffic built by MotivePower, a subsidiary of Wabtec. It has five main variants: MP36PH-3S, MP36PH-3C, MP40PH-3C (supplied to GO of Toronto), MP32PH-Q and MP54AC. The latest model, the MP54AC, is the only one of the types that meets current US emissions standards and is allowed to be sold there for traffic. The streamline single-cab MP40PH-3C, which externally bears some similarities to the EMD F59PHI, features a 16-cylinder EMD 710GB power unit, generating 4,000hp which can haul up to 12 heavy double-decker coaches at speeds of up to 93mph. Sounder Commuter Rail of Seattle also owns three of the locos. GO received 67 of the locomotives between 2007 and 2008. The MotivePower MP40PH-3Cs, from the MPXpress line of locos, were built between 2008 and 2014 and replaced Toronto's GO Transit EMD F59PH fleet between 2011 and 2015. The type is very similar to the MP36PH-3C and MP54 apart from radiator fans and slight variations in radiator layout. On 26 June 2014, 629 arrives at Burlington on a Lakeshore West Line service from Toronto Union.

Chapter 6

Croatia

The national operator is **Hrvatske željeznice (HŽ)**.

Built by Italian manufacturer Breda-Ansaldo, the JŽ Class 362s (HŽ Class 1061) were 3,000V DC B-B-B articulated locomotives, built in two batches: JŽ 362.001-040 (First series, 40 locos, built in 1960–67); and JŽ 362.101-110 (Second series, ten locos, built in 1968). The JŽ locos share many similarities with the FS (Italian) E636 and E646 classes and have an output of 3,540hp and a top speed of 75mph. After the break-up of Yugoslavia, 18 of the fleet went to SŽ and kept their Class 362 classification before being withdrawn in 2009 and replaced by Class 541 new electrics. The remainder of the JŽ 362 fleet went to Croatia and were reclassified as Class 1061. The 1061s were used on the only HŽ 3,000V DC line remaining, the one between Šapjane, Rijeka and Moravice. When this line was converted to 25kV AC in 2012, the Class 1061s were all withdrawn. On 15 February 2012, 1061 012 stands at Rijeke with a service to Zagreb.

With a top speed of 100mph and a rated output of 5,900hp, the Class 1142s (nicknamed 'Brena' after a famous singer) are Croatia's fastest electric locos, holding the rail speed record for the country at 114mph. Sixteen of the type, based on the Swedish Rc family of electric locomotives, were built by the Končar Group between 1981 and 1989 as Class 442s for Yugoslavian railways. All of the fleet were transferred to the Croatian Railways passenger division (HŽ Putnički prijevoz d.o.o.) for use on long-distance traffic. 1142 014 leaves Zagreb on a service to Villach (Austria) on 20 August 2012.

The Croatian Railways Class HŽ 2062s are members of the EMD G26 family of locomotives. Sixty-four of the class were built for Yugoslavian Railways with HŽ inheriting 56 of the fleet. The Slovenian examples are classed as 664s. Twenty of the class were rebuilt by Gredelj and Turner and classified as 2062.1s. With a power output of 2,200hp and a top speed of 77mph, they were staple motive power for much of the hauled traffic on the Croatian network but for the last few years have been relegated to freight duties only with Class 2044s allocated to the remaining passenger duties. On 16 February 2012, 2062 107 arrives at Lovinac on a daytime 'vice' service from Split to Zagreb. The line had been shut by snow for several days and the snow on the cab roof was testament to the deep snowdrifts that the loco had hit in several cuttings; it was quite an experience for the author, who had the view first-hand from the cab.

Powered by a GM 16-645 E3 3,300hp power unit and with a top speed of 75mph, the Class 2063s, nicknamed 'Caravel' (a type of ancient ship), were in later years predominantly freight locomotives. However, they did appear on a number of passenger duties, particularly during electrification work around Rijeka. 2063 007 is shown on one such duty, with a train from Ljubljana, on 14 February 2012. Yugoslav Railways (Jugoslavenske Željeznice) received 14 Class 2063s of the GM GT26CW-2 type from EMD, identifying the locos as Class 663. Other buyers of the off-the-shelf product included Iran, Israel, Morocco, Pakistan, Peru, South Korea and Turkey. The fleet was initially used mainly on freight and passenger trains between Knin and Split, and the whole fleet went to Croatia after the breakup of Yugoslavia in 1991 and were reclassified as 2063s. Some of the fleet has been rebuilt and sold on to Israel Railways with the remaining HŽ 2063s now out of use.

Chapter 7

Czech Republic

The national operator is **České dráhy (ČD)**.

Not strictly a passenger service, the 'Train for Life' was a humanitarian service carrying medical and logistical supplies and three Class 20s for use on rebuilding work that travelled from Derby to Kosovo in 1999, following the Balkans wars. Here, in October 1999, 163 029 pilots 20901, 20902 and 20903 at Svitavy, Czech Republic. The Class 163s, originally designated E 499.3, were 3,000V DC electric locos built by Škoda between 1984 and 1992 and generally used on passenger services. Nicknamed *Peršing* (after the missile), the loco is similar to the Class 162 and is still in service.

The ČSD (latterly after the breakup of Czechoslovakia, ČD and CSSK) introduced two classes of unusual Škoda-built laminated bodyshell electric locos between 1966 and 1969. These were originally Class 499.0 and Class 499.1, later Class 230 and Class 240, with a top speed of 75 and 87mph respectively and an output of 4,130hp. They were given the nickname 'laminátka' and are still in use on Czech and Slovak railways, though in the Czech Republic they are restricted to freight duties. Here, 230 100 awaits its next turn of duty at Brno in July 1990.

Before the new numbering system was completed in the late 1980s, T435 0089 (later renumbered as 720 089) stands at a rural country halt with 84922, a mixed freight/passenger service from Nezamyslice to Morkovice, on 13 February 1992. The Class 720s, or 'Hektors', were built by ČKD between 1958 and 1961 and had a 743hp power unit and a top speed of 38mph. They were mostly used for yard shunting or local trip freights. Export versions were sent to the Soviet Union, East Germany, Iraq, Albania and Cuba.

Class 735s, nicknamed 'Pilštyk' ('Pielstick'), introduced as Class T466 between 1971 and 1979, were built by TSM. Over 300 were produced, but the locos proved largely unsuccessful with many going on to be rebuilt. With a top speed of 56mph and a power output of 1250hp, the type was used mostly on local freight work. The Class 714s were introduced from 1992 as a rebuild of the Class 735 fleet for use on branch-line passenger services. They had a higher top speed of 62mph and are still in service. Some 735s were also rebuilt by ZSR as Class 736s for light mixed-traffic duties. On 14 February 1992, 735 063 stands at Moravske Branice on 84443, the 09.39 to Moravske Branice.

Built between 1977 and 1986 by ČKD as a development of the earlier Class 740 (T448.0), the Class 742, or 'Kocour' ('Tomcat'), was originally classified as T466.2/3 and, with a top speed of 56mph and an output of 1,185hp, was designed primarily for light passenger duties and trip freights. Four hundred and fifty-three examples of the type were produced and some similar locos were also exported to Italy, Serbia and North Korea. Here, 742 330 arrives at Prague Vršovice on a train of double-deck coaches for Čerčany on 3 October 1999.

The Class 753 (steam heat) and 754 (ETH-capable) locos of the ČSD are very popular with Czech enthusiast due to their distinctive looks. Termed 'Brejlovec' ('Goggles'), the ČKD-produced locos are less popular with British cranks due to their heavily silenced power units. The 753s were produced between 1968 and 1977 with a top speed of 62mph and a power output of 1,974hp. The fleet was withdrawn in 2016, though some were converted to Class 750s (ETH capable) and remain in service. 753 022 heads a Karlovy Vary to Decin service in February 1988.

The Class 750s are rebuilt Class 753 (steam-heat 'Goggles', formerly T478.3) that were originally introduced in 1968. They were built by ČKD and 19 examples were converted from steam to electric train heating in the early 1990s. They have a top speed of 62mph and a 2,100hp output. Here, 750 380 stands at Prague *Hlavní Nádraží* (main station) with a service to Turnov on 20 October 1999.

On 13 June 1992, 751 140 stands at Vrane nad Vltavou on train 9015, the 17.03 Prague Vrsovany to Cercany. The locos were nicknamed 'Bardotka' (after Bridget Bardot because of the shape of the cab front) or 'Zamračená' ('Frowners') because of the distinctive cab roof shape. After the two prototypes were produced in 1964 (T478.1001 and T478.1002), production carried on in batches until 1971 with 312 locos of the type eventually being built by ČKD. Under reclassification, no-heat examples were reclassified as Class 752, boiler-fitted examples as Class 751 and ETH-converted locos as Class 749 (T478.2) with 60 being so converted between 1992 and 1996.

On 30 November 1992, T478 1110, later renumbered by ČSD as 751 110, stands at Medzilaborce on train 8645, the 08.27 service from Humenne, with stock comprising DMU trailers. The Class 749, 751 and 752 family of locos are often known as 'Grumpies' by British bashers because of the throaty engine sound made by unsilenced examples (those not fitted with silencers or 'Tlumic' in Czech). The locos have a top speed of 62mph and a 1,500hp power unit installed. Many 751s and 752s are still in use with ČD and ZSSK, particularly ZSSK Cargo, though Class 749s are purely Czech locos (Slovakia carried out no ETH conversions). On ČD the 749s still occasionally appear on passenger services around the Prague area, mostly unsilenced, and are still highly popular with British enthusiasts.

The Class 770s are a type of loco that was also widespread in the Soviet Union and its former allies. Nicknamed 'Cmelak' (or 'Bumblebee' because of its original general ЧМЭ3, translated as ChME3, designation, though it is designated as T669 in Czechoslovakia), the type was sold to Russia (the former USSR), Ukraine, Belarus, Albania, Iraq, India, Syria and the Baltic states. The type still retains some passenger duties in Albania at least. 8,200 examples were built by ČKD between the prototype in 1963 and the last export models in 1994 and they feature a straight six-cylinder ČKD 1,300hp power unit and a top speed of 56mph. The production of ČSD locos of type T669 was subcontracted to SMZ in Dubnica (Slovakia) between 1967 and 1969. Unsilenced, the locos are vaguely reminiscent of a UK Class 20, though their appearances on passenger duties were rare in the Czech and Slovak Republics, save for one booked turn on the branch from Vranany to Luzec. The similar T669.1 Class became Class 770 under the new ČSD classification scheme. On 1 September 1992, 770 001 prepares to leave Vranany on train 96970, the 15.04 to Luzec. This 2-mile-long branch line is now closed. The rolling stock is a four-wheeled coach, heated by a centrally placed coal-fired stove (a relatively common arrangement in eastern and central Europe until the 1980s).

Chapter 8

Denmark

The national operator is **Danske Statsbaner (DSB)**.

Thirty-one Henschel ME Class Co-Co diesel-electrics were produced between 1981 and 1985 for DSB for use on regional passenger services. With a GM E645E3B power unit rated at 3,300hp, the locos have a rated maximum speed of 109mph. Around 30 of the locos are still in traffic. However, they are due to be replaced by electric locos in 2021. On 31 August 2001, ME1536 (in original DSB black/red) and ME1552 (in newer dark blue) stand at Odense on a service from Copenhagen to Århus.

Chapter 9

France

The national operator is **Société Nationale des Chemins de fer Français (SNCF).**

In 1985, SNCF BB 7200 Class 'Nez Cassée' ('Broken Nose') 7290 stands at Aix-Les-Bains on an international service from Spain, via Paris, using Talgo stock. Between 1976 and 1985, 240 of the mixed-traffic BB 7200s were built by Alsthom and MTE. Some of the class were fitted for 125mph running, though the majority, including 7290, were restricted to 100mph from their 5,450hp power output. The 'Broken Nose' family included the bi-current BB 22200s and BB 15000s and were a development of earlier classes, including CC 6500, CC 21000, CC 72000 and CC 40100. Around 100 locos remain in traffic with SNCF.

Nicknamed 'Danseuses' ('Dancers'), 105 of the Alsthom-built BB 17000 locos were introduced between 1965 and 1968 to work mixed-traffic duties before settling on suburban passenger services in and around Paris, the 'trains de la banlieue'. They have a top speed of 56 or 87mph and a power output of 3,940hp. Now owned and operated by Transilien (SNCF's suburban rail provider) they are still concentrated in the Paris area though are now being replaced by Alstom's new Prima locos.

SNCF Class BB 22200 number 22393 stands at Paris Gare Du Nord on a train for Calais in 1986. The class, 205 of which were produced by Alsthom between 1976 and 1986, belongs to a family of similarly shaped Alstom locos, which include the SNCF BB 7200 and BB 15000 classes, produced for many railways throughout Europe. Some modified examples have a top speed of 125mph and an output of 7,510hp for use on TGV lines, while the remainder are 5,850hp with a top speed of 100mph. Until the introduction of Class 92s, nine of the class appeared in Kent on Channel Tunnel freight services. They were designated as Class 22s in the UK and worked until 1995.

Between 1968 and 1971, 106 examples of the SNCF 66400 Class locos were built by Alstom, Compagnie Électro-Mécanique, SACM and Fives-Lille. With an output of 1,400hp and a top speed of 75mph, they were initially widely used on passenger services. On 16 October 1999, 66432 and an unidentified partner wait at Auxerre on a Paris service. Some of the fleet were overhauled and re-engined with MTU power units between 2004 and 2010, becoming Class BB 69400. Some 66400s are still in limited use with SNCF on engineering duties.

The SNCF Class 67400, built by Brissonneau and Lotz between 1969 and 1975, was the final development of the BB 67000 Class and is probably the most familiar loco to British visitors. Two hundred and two examples were built, and they operate freight and passenger services all over France. Powered by a 2,367hp Pielstick power unit and numbered 67401–67632 they have a top speed of 87mph. 67581 stands at Calais Ville with a local service to Boulogne on 17 February 2006. These services are now wholly operated by EMUs. Many members of the class are still in operation today though their numbers, and their passenger diagrams, are greatly reduced.

Chapter 10

Germany

The national operator is **Deutsche Bahn AG (DB or DBAG)**.

The DB Class 103 is an iconic Co-Co electric locomotive designed for high-speed passenger service, particularly along the Rhine line, where a powerful loco was needed to accelerate after the many speed restrictions along the route. Manufactured by a consortium, including AEG, Brown Boveri & Cie, Henschel, Krauss-Maffei, Krupp and Siemens AG, the production locos had a rated continuous output of 7,980hp and a top speed of 125mph with 103 003 and 103 222 modified to allow speeds of up to 174mph. The speed record for the class was achieved by 103 118 in 1985, when it reached 176mph. With outputs of up to 16,000hp recorded (later the output was limited to 12,000hp) these are the most powerful single-unit locomotives ever built. Following the construction of four prototypes in 1965 a further 145 locos were outshopped between 1970 and 1973. On 18 February 1992, 103 133 waits at St. Polten on train EC61, the overnight sleeper service from Munich to Vienna. Class 103s regularly worked international services through to the Austrian capital.

On 3 April 2010, 103 235 approaches Bullay on a train from Koblenz to Trier during the DB 175-year anniversary celebrations along the Mosel Valley, between Trier, Saarbrucken, Gerolstein and Koblenz. The preserved 103 was hauling a full Rheingold set, including a piano bar. Although most of the fleet was withdrawn in 2003, replaced by newer loco types like the Class 101s, together with the ICE EMUs, 17 of the locos have been preserved with five in main-line serviceable condition, which is testament to the popularity of the type. These remaining locos are used occasionally on service trains with the odd booked turn, particularly for the remaining Frankfurt-based locos. Two of the main-line certified locos are still used by DB for infrastructure and rolling stock testing purposes.

The Class 111, built by Krauss-Maffei, Henschel, Krupp, Siemens, AEG and BBC between 1974 and 1984, was seen as an upgrade to, and probable replacement for, the Class 110, though the 110s soldiered on for many years after the introduction of the Class111s. With a top speed of 100mph (upgraded for intercity work) and an output of 4,990hp, 227 of the locos were built, and most are still in service. Class 111s could be found on a wide range of passenger work throughout Western Germany but today are largely restricted to suburban (S-Bahn) and regional duties. They are due to be withdrawn over the next few years as DB receives a large number of new EMUs. On 5 June 2010, 111 115 is seen at Cologne Hbf on an RB service to Aachen.

On 24 February 1991, 142 005 stands at Dresden Hauptbahnof on double-decker stock with an S5 (Stadtbahn – route 5) service to Tharandt. Originally designated as E42, 292 of the Class 242 electrics were built by LEW Henningsdorf from 1963 and were generally used on freight traffic and some local services because of their top speed of only 62mph. Together with the Class 211 electrics, the types were nicknamed 'Holzroller' or 'Wood Rollers'. The locos became classes 109 and 142 under the reunified DB (from 1992) and were withdrawn from traffic by the end of the noughties.

On 19 September 1990, 150 171 is at Geislingen on train 5235, the 10.14 Plochingen–Ulm, a rare passenger diagram for the generally freight-only Class 150s. The type was originally designated as Class E 50, Class 150 from 1968, and designed as a heavy freight locomotive to replace the last of DB's freight steam locos. Between 1957 and 1973, 157 of the 128t Co-Co locos were built by Krupp, AEG, BBC, Henschel and Krauss-Maffei, and they had an output of 6,000hp and a top speed of 62mph. After a successful career the fleet was withdrawn by DB in 2002, and two of the class have been preserved.

The 95-strong fleet of DR Class 211s, built by LEW Hennigsdorf from 1962 to1964 with a power output of 3,935hp and a top speed of 75mph, was originally classified as E11 under DR but was reclassified as Class 109 under DBAG. The fleet was withdrawn in 1994. 211 013 stands at Leipzig Hbf on an empty stock working in 1991.

A busy scene at Berlin Lichtenberg on 19 September 1999 as 140 629, dragging 20901, 20902 and 20903 on the 'Train for Life' to Kosovo, waits the road for a non-stop run to Dresden. In the adjoining Platform 17, 'Trabbi' 143 851 awaits with a regional train to Eberswalde, RB39282, the 16.24 departure. The Class 140s, together with Class 139s, were originally classified as E40, a German standard electric or 'Einheits-Elektrolokomotiven', with most duties being freight-based as opposed to the passenger Class 110s. Between March 1957 and August 1973, 879 were built by Krupp, Henschel, Krauss-Maffei, Siemens, AEG and BBC. They have a top speed of 68mph and a power output of 5,000hp. The fleet was replaced by classes 145, 185 and 189 in the noughties.

The Class 143s, previously numbered 243s under the Deutsche Reichsbahn, have been a very reliable and successful Bo-Bo electric locomotive with many examples still in service today. With a rated output of 5,000hp and a top speed of 75mph, 636 of the locos were built for DR between 1982 and 1990 by VEB Lokomotivbau und Elektrotechnische Werke (LEW Hennigsdorf). The type went on to see service in the west on local push-pull passenger workings after reunification. Recent EMU introductions have seen the number of 143s in service reduced greatly and the whole fleet of 'Trabbis' is likely to be withdrawn in the next few years, though many examples are still in use with private freight operators. Here, 243 308 stands with double-decker stock at Rostock on 17 March 1991.

Almost 30 years after my first visit to Germany, by 2015 the railways of the, by now reunified, country had changed dramatically. With ME 146 03 on a southbound train, in the background a 'Trabbi' Class 114 (100mph upgrade of the Class 143) moved over from the former East can be seen on a regional service at Hamburg Hauptbahnhof on 21 June 2015. The local authority-owned Metronom company took over the Regional Express services between Hamburg and Bremen from DB. The 31-strong Class 146 fleet was built by Adtranz between 1997 and 2002 and has an output of 5,600hp and a top speed of 100mph.

The DR Class 250s, reclassified as Class 155s under the reunified DB, were built between 1974 and 1984 with 273 of the locos eventually being introduced. Constructed by LEW Hennigsdorf, the Co-Cos are a powerful design, rated at 7,200hp with a top speed of 75mph. The type was initially used on some heavier passenger services but eventually settled down on heavy freight work and occasional regional passenger duties, as shown here where 155 016 can be seen at Berlin Lichtenberg on 19 September 1999. The design proved very reliable and today many of the locos are still in service with DB Schenker, Germany's main rail freight operator.

Originally classified as E 251, later Class 251 and finally under DBAG, Class 171, these locos were used exclusively on the Blankenburg (Harz)–Königshütte (Rübeland Railway) line and were electrified at 25kV and 50Hz, as opposed to the standard German 15kV and 16⅔Hz. In 1965, 15 of the locos were built by LEW and had an output of 4,400hp and a top speed of 50mph. Passenger operations for the class ended in 2000 because of the lack of train door opening facilities, and the fleet was withdrawn from freight workings in 2004. On 10 June 1991, 251 011 worked trains 16436, the 12.31 Blankenberg–Konigshütte, and 16437, the 13.50 Konigshütte–Blankenberg. Here, the DR veteran is seen at Konigshütte on the return working.

185618 waits at Numburg on a regional working on 18 February 2012. Bombardier introduced the marketing name TRAXX (Transnational Railway Applications with eXtreme fleXibility) for their latest diesel and electric loco designs. The locos share similar bodyshells, bogies and AC traction motors, and many variants have been sold to a wide range of operators throughout Europe. Final assembly of the locos is completed in Bombardier's plants in Kassel and Vado Ligure. The dual-voltage Class 185, dubbed 'Europalok', shares many features with the Class 145 family. The marketing name for the 185 was TRAXX F140 AC, and the DB 185s were delivered between 2001 and 2003. The Swiss locos (used by SBB Cargo) are classified as Re482 and those used by the BLS as Re485. Many Class 185s are also used by German private freight operators and hire companies. TRAXX locomotives are assembled and tested at Bombardier's plant in Kassel, Germany, with the exception of the DC-only versions which are assembled at Vado Ligure. The Class 185s have a top speed of 87mph and a rated output of 7,500hp.

The Deutsche Reichsbahn Class V100s, like the DB V100s, were centre cab light mixed-traffic Bo-Bos. Between 1966 and 1985, 1,145 locos in the V100 family were built by LEW Heningsdorf, with 110 production (867 locos) ceasing in 1978. The Class 112s were Class 110s, re-engined at Stendal from 1972, with new power units that produced 1,184hp and a top speed that remained at 62mph. Almost 500 locomotives were converted to Class 112s. Following reunification, the 112s became Class 202s under DBAG. The fleet was withdrawn by DR in the noughties with many being supplied to private industry. LEW also supplied some V100s to China and industrial operators in Czechoslovakia. 112 322 arrives at Gera Sud on a train from Glauchau on 27 February 1991.

Class 114s were 1,500hp re-engined versions of the 987hp Class 110s, built by LEW and modified in 1972. They went on to become DBAG Class 204s after reunification. On 21 September 1990, DR centre cab 114 359 is detached from train E2054, the 06.24 Halle–Cologne Hbf. Class 110 110 505 worked the train forward. Not too long after the fall of the Berlin Wall, this was quite a spectacular incursion into the West by a smaller main-line DR loco more used to local passenger and freight work in the GDR. Rough riding at speed meant that DBAG restricted the 204s to 50mph, hastening their demise.

The Class 118s (originally V180s) were DR's largest diesel locomotives when introduced in 1960 and shared a number of physical and mechanical similarities with DB's V200 'Warships', including their Voith diesel hydraulic transmission. Over 300 examples were built by Lokomotivbau Karl Marx Babelsberg between 1963 and 1970. Like other 'Warship'-type designs, they were powered by two high-speed power units, in this case VEB 12 KVD 18/21-A1s delivering 900hp each. The later series of locos were delivered as C-Cs for branch line use. The type was gradually replaced on heavier freight and express passenger workings by the Russian Class 132 design and the fleet was withdrawn by DB in the mid-90s, though many have gone on to see use with private freight operators. On 8 May 1991, 118 731 is seen at Bad Doberan on 15126, the 11.35 Wismar to Rostock.

On 23 February 1991, 118 578 waits departure from Berlin Wannsee on 11511, the 08.42 to Potsdam Hbf.

DR's Class 119 diesel hydraulics were a development of the Class 118s, with ETH, produced in Romania by the 23rd August Locomotive Works of Bucharest. As a result of Comecon trade agreements, the GDR was not allowed to construct diesel locos over 1,500hp, and the only available locos from the USSR were the larger Class 130, 132 and 142 types. The Romanians agreed to supply the notoriously unreliable Class 119s, known as 'Sorgenkind' ('Problem Children'), the major issue of which was their hydraulic transmission. Between 1976 and 1985, 200 were built but the ongoing problems saw the fleet retired by 2006. 119 194 is seen on a regional double-decker service on DR in 1990.

A number of variants of the DB Class V100s were built, designated as V100.10 and V100.20, later to become Class 211, 212 and 213. Between 1958 and 1963, 364 Class 211s were built by MaK. With an output of 1,085hp and a top speed of 62mph, the steam-heat hydraulics were used on many branch-line passenger services before being replaced by DMUs throughout the 1990s. The last examples of the class were withdrawn by DB in 2001. Many examples were transferred to private operators after the fleet withdrawal and ÖBB also bought some of the withdrawn locos in the 90s and noughties and classified them as Class 2048. On 8 August 1989, 211 019 sits at Roth after arrival on 6218, the 18.09 from Hilpolstein.

The V100.20 Class (later Class 212) was the longest surviving member of the V100 family, being a later, higher-powered version of the V100.10 (Class 211) intended for some main-line use rather than just branch-line duties. Between 1962 and 1965, 381 of the locos were built by MaK. The loco had a 1,338hp power unit and a top speed of 62mph. The DB fleet was withdrawn (by freight operator Railion) in 2004 with many examples being transferred to private operators for infrastructure duties; nine locomotives were preserved. 212067 is seen here on a peak-time commuter working.

The Class 213s were a variant of the MaK-built V100.20 Class and the last ten locos in the production series were outshopped with stronger brakes and modified hydraulic drives for use on steeper-graded lines. These last ten locos became Class 213s after DB's 1968 renumbering, and the rest were classified as 212s. The Class 213s became heavily associated with the steeply graded Boppard–Emmelshausen line (the steepest adhesion worked line in West Germany, which climbs 1,100ft in only 4 miles at a gradient of 1 in 16.4). Between 1983 and 1995, Class 213s operated trains on this branch, starting on the west bank of the Rhine. On 9 August 1989, 213 337 sits at Boppard with train 7575, the 11.32 to Emmelshausen.

Originally designated as V160s (renamed after 1968), DB's Class 216s 1,873hp, 75mph MTU-powered diesel hydraulics were developed largely by Krupp and Henschel and were the forerunners of other members of the V160 family, including Classes 210, 215, 217, 218 and 219. Two hundred and twenty-four of these steam-heat locos were produced, and there were over 800 examples of the V160 family overall. The V160s used a single high-powered diesel power unit, as opposed to the V200s which relied on two, smaller, high-speed Maybachs. Some Class 216s are still in use with private freight operators in Germany. The steam-heat Class 216s were replaced by more powerful ETH-capable Class 218s, losing their passenger diagrams during the 1990s, and the type was eventually withdrawn by DB in 2004. In common with other DB diesel locomotives, the Class 216s were delivered in altrot (old red) livery, which was replaced in the 1970s by ocean blue/beige colours. From the end of the 1980s, locos were repainted in orientrot livery (red with a white cab front panel). 216 173 at Hessisch Olbendorf on E3728, the 17.49 Hildesheim–Bielefeld, on 7 August 1989.

The German V200 Class diesel hydraulics (Class 220 from 1968) were very popular with British enthusiasts, largely due to their family similarity with BR's 'Warship' hydraulics. Between 1956 and 1968, 86 of the locos were built by Krauss-Maffei and MaK (after production of five prototypes in 1953). The two Maybach V12 power units gave a combined output of 2,170hp and had a top speed of 87mph. In 1962, the V200.1 (later, Class 221), a more powerful version of the V200, was introduced. Following withdrawal of DB's fleet in 1984, many were sold on to foreign operators in Italy, Greece, France and Switzerland. On 6 June 2010, V200 033 waits at Reinbach with one of a number of additional workings between Bonn Hbf and Reinbach that were operated in conjunction with a festival day at the branch station. The loco returned with the stock as a train to Hagen later in the day.

On 9 May 1991, 218 274 ventures into the old East Germany at Gardelegen on an IC service from the west. The Class 218 was DB's standard large mixed-traffic main-line diesel hydraulic and worked most of their heavier express and regional diesel-hauled passenger services from the 1970s into the noughties. Today, the class still has a large number of freight and passenger diagrams throughout the country. Built by Krupp, Henschel, Krauss-Maffei and MaK between 1968 and 1979, and originally classified as V164, 12 prototypes were produced, together with 398 production models. The type was the final development of the V160 family of locos, which included Classes 215, 216 and 217. Re-engining has seen many of the fleet have their original 2,500hp MTU TB10 power units replaced with 2,800hp TB11s; the top speed remained as 87mph. Some other locos have had a 2,700hp Pielstick unit installed.

On 20 February 2011, push-pull-fitted 218 402 propels a regional service for Ulm. The earlier series locos (up to 218 399) were withdrawn by 2003 with the later 218.4s (as here) being retained for regional and suburban push-pull use. Around 200 of the fleet (50 per cent of those built) remain active, including the 218.8 sub-class which was modified for dragging ICEs. Class 245s were due to replace the 'Rabbits' (named for their exhaust deflector 'ears') in the last few years but problems with the new locomotives could see the 218s last for a few more years to come.

Russian-built 232 221 stands under the roof at Dresden Hbf with a service to Zittau on 24 February 1991. The Class 130 family, Classes 130–132, later 232–234 under DBAG, were built by the October Revolution Locomotive Works at Luhansk, Ukraine, between 1973 and 1982. Seven hundred and nine of the ETH-fitted Class 132s, nicknamed 'Ludmilla', were built, making it the most numerous class of diesel locos on DR. Powered by a Kolomna 5D49 power unit giving out 3,000hp, they have a top speed of 75mph and they powered most of the longer-distance diesel hauled passenger services in East Germany. Their rugged reliability led to many of them seeing use with DBAG (they were renumbered as Class 232 after reunification) with some still in service on freight duties with private operators.

The DR Class 142 is one of a family of over 700 Soviet-built diesel locos produced for the GDR in Luhansk, now part of Ukraine, between 1973 and 1982. The type, nicknamed 'Ludmilla', also includes DR Classes 130, 131 and 132 and later DB-modified Classes 233, 234 and 241. Similar locos were sold to Bulgaria, Czechoslovakia and the USSR itself. Six higher-powered examples were produced in 1977 for heavy freight. The 4,000hp, 62mph Class 142s were reliable and successful, though increased electrification saw the need for these locos end and they were transferred to private ownership, primarily Schauffele of Cottbus, by DBAG. On 17 March 1991, 142 004 arrives at Rovershagen on E415, the 14.32 Greifswald–Rostock, a fill-in turn between its usual heavy steel freight traffic duties.

Over 400 examples were built of the DB Class 290 (originally V90), a heavy-duty diesel hydraulic shunter and light freight loco. Originally classified as V90s, the 100 Class 290s form part of a family that includes Classes 291, 294, 295 and 296. Built by Mak München between 1963 and 1974 with a top speed of 43mph and output of 1,100hp (290 001-020) or 50mph and an output of 1,350hp (290 021 and later), the locos are a development of the smaller V100s. Since 2003, the class has been refitted with MTU power units and renumbered in the 290 5xx range. The type saw very little passenger use, though one famous turn, where a 290 piloted a local passenger train to save a path to the end of a branch line before working a freight service back, was the 17.29 Roth–Hilpolstein. On 1 August 1989, 290 359 is seen on 6217, the departure from Roth, with 211 059 on the rear.

The DE 2700 Class was built by Siemens in 1997 for NSB, designated as Di6 in Norway, and used mostly on freight services. With a number of technical faults (including bogie problems, high fuel use and computer failures in low temperatures) hindering their availability, the fleet was returned to Germany in 1999 and eventually leased to NOB (Nord-Ostsee-Bahn) for regional passenger use on Schleswig–Holstein routes (north of Hamburg to Sylt). With a 3550hp MaK V12 power unit and a top speed of 100mph, the 12 locos in the fleet have never been used to their full potential. This typical rural view of a stopping service from Hamburg Altona operated by NOB was captured on 21 June 2015.

During the April 2010 Dampfspektakel, T11 7512 (74 231), together with shunter 261 761 in the consist and 58 311 bringing up the rear, arrives at Daun, on the line between Gerolstein and Ulmen, with a Plandampf working on 2 April. The Prussian T11 2-6-0T tank engines were built between 1903 and 1910 by Union Gießerei of Borsig for Berlin suburban passenger traffic, and 470 were constructed. Though rated at only 500hp, but with a top speed of 50mph, the T11s showed a useful turn of speed on light 'Stadtbahn' work. Under the Deutsche Reichsbahn, from 1925, the type became Class 74.0-3 and locos were allocated numbers 74 001–358. Most of the fleet were withdrawn by the end of 1960, after a gradual rundown of the class, as urban passenger networks around the main German cities became electrified. Two of the fleet were preserved; 7512 at the Minden Museum railway and the former 74 104 (designated Class PKP Oki1) in Poland.

The Class 41 steam locos were standard ('Einheitslok') 2-8-2 freight engines. Between 1937 and 1941, 366 were built by various manufacturers, including BMAG, Borsig, Maschinenfabrik Esslingen, Henschel & Sohn, Arnold Jung Lokomotivfabrik, Krauss-Maffei, Krupp, Orenstein & Koppel and Schichau. Officially withdrawn by DR as late as 1988 (41 1231 being the last example in service), these were some of the last steam locos in use in the former East Germany. They had been rebuilt with fresh boilers after the war and termed 'Rekoloks', proving themselves to be reliable and versatile on a wide range of duties, including heavy freight and fast express services. On 9 May 1991, 41 1231 can be seen paired with 44 1486 at Haldesleben on 6448, the 15.40 Magdeburg Hbf to Oebisfelde. 41 1231 is today preserved at Staßfurt depot and awaits overhaul.

The Class 44 was a 2-10-0 heavy-goods three-cylindered standard steam loco, or 'Einheitsdampflokomotive', with a top speed of 50mph. Between 1926 and 1949, 1,989 examples were built by a wide range of manufacturers throughout Europe, including BMAG, Borsig, Batignolles-Châtillon, Henschel & Sohn, LOFAG, Krauss-Maffei, Krupp, ME, Krenau, Schneider-Creusot and Schichau. Following the end of the Second World War, the surviving locomotives were inherited by, or given as reparations to, DB, DR, ČSD, ÖBB, PKP (as Ty4s) and the SNCF. On 10 May 1991, 44 1486 awaits departure from Magdeburg with train 6448, the 15.40 to Oebisfelde. Two Class 44s are in operational condition currently. 44 1486 has been preserved at Staßfurt and 44 1593 is with the Veluwsche Stoomtrein Maatschappij (VSM) in Beekbergen, Netherlands; many others have been preserved.

The Deutsche Reichsbahn Class 50 was a 2-10-0 freight steam loco ('Einheitslok') with over 3,000 examples built between 1939 and 1959. The type was very successful, being produced widely by many manufacturers throughout occupied Europe, and production continued until 1959 in Romania (for export to China and North Korea). See page 44 (as per Classes 41 and 44) for list of factories producing DR locos in occupied Europe. Following the end of the Second World War, many locos were used in the countries they remained in after hostilities ceased (e.g. they were designated as Ty5 in Poland). Built in 1942 by BMAG, 50 3606, one of 208 examples, was part of the DR 50.35 'Reko' ('Rebuilt') loco class, a type that remained in service on DR until 1987. On 9 May 1991, the loco leaves Gardelegen on train 9425, the 11.58 from Oebisfelde to Rathenow. The loco is today preserved at Staßfurt depot but is not operational.

The Class 65.10s were a class of 88 2-8-4T steam locos produced between 1954 and 1957 by DR at VEB Lokomotivbau Karl Marx Babelsberg (LKM, formerly Orenstein & Koppel) for suburban commuter traffic. The fleet was replaced by Class 118s and lighter diesels in the 1970s, and the last of the fleet was withdrawn in 1977. On 9 May 1991, 65 1049 leaves Haldesleben on the empties after working 6451, the 15.08 from Oebisfelde. Today this loco is preserved at the Chemnitz Hilbersdorf depot.

99 1784 is a standard design ('Neubeaulokomotiven') of Class 99.77-79, ordered by the Deutsche Reichsbahn after the Second World War for the Saxony narrow-gauge lines. Built by VEB Lokomotivbau Karl Marx Babelsberg in 1953, 750mm-gauge 2-10-2T 99 1784 is now based at the Rügensche Kleinbahn (often known as the 'Rasender Roland') at Putbus, on the island of Rugen on the north-eastern Baltic coast of Germany. The line runs 16 miles from Putbus to Gohren. Privatised in 1996, the railway is now run as a tourist operation. 99 1784 was originally based on the Radebeul-Ost to Radeburg line (near Dresden) and was moved to the island in the early 1980s. With a top speed of 19mph, the loco is ideally suited to its new life in preservation. Here, 99 1784 prepares to leave Gohren on 23 June 2015.

The 99.73–76 Class of 750mm-gauge 2-10-2T steam locomotives, 32 of which were built between 1928 and 1933 for the Deutsche Reichsbahn by Sachsische Maschinenfabrik and Berliner Maschinenbau, for use in Saxony, were designated as a standard design, or 'Einheitslokomotiven'. With a top speed of 19mph and a power output of 590hp, the design was very successful working the hilly routes such as Hainsberg–Kipsdorf, Cranzahl–Oberwiesenthal and Zittau–Oybin/Jonsdorf. Some of the locos are still in use today on the preserved operations at Zittau and Freital-Hainsberg. In February 1991, 099 736 stands at Freital-Hainsberg on a timetabled service to Kurort Kipsdorf.

99 1758 is a Type 99.7 2-10-2 750mm-gauge steam loco built by BMAG Schwartzkopff of Berlin in 1933 for use on the lines around Zittau (in south-east Saxony, near the borders with the Czech Republic and Poland). On 26 February 1991, 99 1758 is seen at Bertsdorf, famous for its simultaneous departures to the terminus stations of Jonsdorf and Oybin, on 14180, the 12.10 Zittau to Kurort Jonsdorf. The loco is today preserved by the Saxon Oberlausitz Railway Company (Zittauer Schmalspurbahn) for use on the now-preserved line and is still serviceable.

On 28 February 1991, Class 99.23 metre-gauge steam loco 99 7244 waits to depart from Wernigerode with 14447, the 15.14 to Beneckenstein, while retro-numbered 99247 moves off shed. Built by DR at VEB Lokomotivbau 'Karl Marx' Babelsberg between 1954 and 1956, 17 of the 700hp 2-10-2T Neubaulokomotive (new build locos), with a top speed of 25mph, were used on the Harz network. Originally numbered 99 231 to 99 247, they were renumbered 99 7231 to 99 7247 in 1970. Both locos are still intact, though 7244 is out of service.

On 28 February 1991, 99 7238 approaches Wernigerode Westerntor. The Harz network was taken over on 1 February 1993 by the Harzer Schmalspurbahnen GmbH (HSB), with shareholders formed from the local authorities along the routes, and is now essentially a preserved operation. Wernigerode is the main headquarters, depot and workshops and the HSB today is still Germany's largest narrow-gauge network with a total track length of 87 miles.

Chapter 11

Hungary

The national operator is **Magyar Államvasutak (MÁV)**.

The V43 Class were built by Hungarian manufacturer Ganz for MÁV, with 379 locos being built between 1963 and 1982. The initial design proposal came from a consortium of European manufacturers, termed the 50 C/s Group, formed of ACEC, AEG-Telefunken, Alsthom, Brown Boveri, Siemens, SLM, Oerlikon and Matériel de Traction Électrique. The group was also partially responsible for the design of electric locos in Korea, South Africa and Turkey, together with the Portuguese CP 2500 Class. The V43s became the mainstay of Hungarian passenger haulage and still provide the bulk of regional and local passenger services today though they are being replaced by more modern types such as the Bombardier TRAXX electric locos. The locos are rated at 3,000hp with a top speed of 75mph. Reclassification since 2011 has seen the three sub-series renumbered as follows: V43.1 – Class 431; V43.2 – Class 432; V43.3 – Class 433. V43 1100 waits at Budapest on a regional service on 17 August 2012.

The MÁV Class M47 locomotives, nicknamed 'Dacia' because of their Romanian background, were built between 1974 and 1975 at the Malaxa 23rd August Works in Bucharest. They feature 700hp Maybach-Mercedes diesel hydraulic power units, a top speed of 22/44mph and were designed for local passenger, freight and shunting duties. There were three sub series, /0, /1 and /2, with 113 locomotives being built in total, the last series of which featured ETH for passenger work. Here, M47 2041 is seen at Szombathely after arrival on train 9835, the 11.10 from Zalagerzeg, on 9 June 1992.

Hungary was out of step with many Iron Curtain countries in the 1950s and needed to buy new locomotives (as the country became more industrialised). MÁV considered buying Maybach-powered German V200s or the General Motors-engined Nohab diesel-electrics being built under licence by Nydqvist & Holm AB ('NoHAB') in Trollhättan, Sweden. After deciding on the diesel-electric design, the M61s were delivered between 1963 and 1964 and went on to become a great success. Seven of the type are preserved in Hungary. M61 008 pauses at a rural halt on train 950, the 06.35 Budapest Deli–Zalaegerzeg, on 9 June 1992.

The standard Nohab diesel-electrics, produced by Nydqvist & Holm AB of Sweden and based on EMD's F-Units, were introduced in many countries around Europe in the early 1960s. MÁV ordered 20 of the locos, which were delivered in 1963 and 1964 and proved highly successful. The 1,700hp locos had a top speed of 65mph and the last members of the fleet were withdrawn from regular traffic in November 2000, though several have been preserved and see occasional use on service trains. MÁV Nohab M61 020 waits at Székesfehérvár on train 9716, the 15.30 Budapest Deli–Tapolca, on 10 June 1992.

The M62s, nicknamed 'Sergeis', have been a widely used loco type behind the Iron Curtain. Between 1965 and 1979, over 7,000 were built in the USSR at the October Revolution Locomotive Plant in Voroshilovgrad, with Hungary's M62 001 being the first, and they also served in Cuba, North Korea and Mongolia. From 1997 onwards, 34 of the total 288 MÁV examples had their Kolomna power units replaced by Caterpillar versions and they were redesignated as Class 628.3. On 9 June 1992, three classes of MÁV diesel locos wait to depart Zalaegerszeg on passenger trains with M62 215 on train 954, the 12.54 Szombathely–Budapest Déli. Meanwhile, M41 2193 and M47 2041 wait in adjoining platforms with local services.

Chapter 12

Ireland

The national operator is **Iarnród Éireann (IE)**.

The Córas Iompair Éireann 181s, a class of 12 locos originally numbered B181 to B192, were built in 1966 by General Motors Electro-Motive Division (EMD) at La Grange, Illinois. They have a top speed of 75mph. They differ from the earlier, but very similar, Class 141s by having a slightly higher-rated power unit – an EMD 8-645E engine of 1,100hp compared to the original EMD 8-567CR engine of 960hp fitted in the 141s. Together the 141s and 181s are nicknamed 'Baby GMs' and were often used in pairs within and between classes. The fleet was withdrawn in 2009 and one loco has been preserved (190). On 10 June 2004, 187 waits at Ennis with one Cravens coach and a steam-heat generator van on a service to Limerick.

The Córas Iompair Éireann 071s are a fleet of 18 locos built by GM between 1976 and 1988. They feature an EMD JT22CW power unit giving 2,250hp and a top speed of 90mph. The fleet lost their passenger duties in the noughties though a refurbishment program, started in 2013, should ensure their use on freight for many years to come. The locos are still particular favourites on charter and railtour duties. GM supplied three similar locos for Northern Ireland Railways (the Class 111s) and also four Class 666s (with flatter-sided bodyshells) for Yugoslavia, which have now been inherited by Serbia. Class 071s were particularly popular with UK enthusiasts and they stood in for the booked Class 201s on a wide range of duties in the 90s and noughties and put in some excellent performances on IE's remaining Cravens, Mark 2 and Mark 3 stock. On 3 October 2003, 088 stands at Galway on a service to Dublin Heuston.

Chapter 13

Italy

Trenitalia is the main state-owned train operator in Italy and is part of Ferrovie dello Stato Italiane.

The Class E464 was built between 1999 and 2015 and 717 locomotives were produced. The fleet was originally manufactured by ABB Trazione, then ADTranz, and finally Bombardier after a series of takeovers. Operating from the standard Italian 3,000V DC with an output of 4,700hp and a top speed of 100mph, they are the standard loco for suburban passenger services. Single-cabbed electric E464 538 stands on the blocks at Milan Central on 26 February 2011.

The FS E.652 Class, introduced in 1989, was derived from the E.633/2 classes and forms a group of B-B-B electric locos operating on 3,000V DC supply and is nicknamed 'Tigre' or 'Tiger'. Built by a range of Italian companies, with a top speed of 99mph and an output of 5,600hp, the locos proved very useful on passenger traffic, particularly in northern Italy. Since 2017, the remaining 171 E.652s have been allocated to the Global Logistic (Cargo) division of Trenitalia. E652 093 stands at Brennero on the evening of 26 February 2011.

The D.445 Class locos are a Fiat-built B-B monomotor type, developed from the earlier D.443 and produced between 1974 and 1988. With a 1,924hp Fiat A210-12 power unit and a top speed of 81mph, the 150-strong fleet was responsible for most of Italy's diesel-hauled passenger services and still retains a small number of passenger diagrams for the 80 or so surviving locos in service. D445 1124 is seen approaching Venice Mestre (the junction station for the famous city) on 26 February 2011.

Chapter 14
Kosovo

The national operators are:

Albanian – **Hekurudhat e Kosovës**.
Serbian – **Železnice Kosova** is the national railway company of Kosovo.

In January 2001, four ex-Norwegian Di3 locos, 3 619, 3 633, 3 641 and 3 643 were bought by the Norwegian Government and sent via the UN as a donation to Kosovo to help rebuild their railway system after the Balkans War. Many different locomotives were donated to Hekurudhat e Kosovës/Železnice Kosova by other European countries though the Nohabs appear to have performed better than most in the minimal maintenance and spares environment, with one of them, 007, surviving in traffic until 2017. In possibly the least lavish railway station in any capital city in Europe (Priština), Nohab 001 (ex-Di3 641, later renumbered as 2640 003) stands after arrival from Pej with a generator car for ETH and two donated ex-ÖBB coaches on 17 January 2013. The several hours return trip cost the grand sum of around two Euros.

Chapter 15

Lithuania

The national operator is **Lietuvos geležinkeliai (LG)**.

The TEP70 (ТЭП70) is a Russian-built diesel-electric locomotive with a 3,975hp output from its Kolomna type 2A-5D49, four-stroke V16 and a top speed of 100mph. It has been built for the 1,520mm (4ft 11$^{27}/_{32}$ in) Russian gauge. Introduced in 1973 with inspiration from the 4,000hp Kestrel prototype imported from the UK, the class was widely used throughout the former Soviet Union and is still in service in Belarus, Estonia, Russia, Ukraine, Latvia, Lithuania and Kazakhstan. On 5 June 2012, TEP 70 0345 is at the head of train 0169, the 09.41 Vilnius to Klaipeda, awaiting departure from the Lithuanian capital with a Lietuvos geležinkeliai (LG) service. An attendant at each door lowers steps to welcome the passenger on board in true Eastern Bloc style.

The TEP 70BS is a modern development of the TEP70 with modern electronics, including AC transmission, and was also built at the Kolomna Locomotive Works. TEP 70 BS 002 arrives at Klaipeda on a train from Vilnius on 6 June 2012. The TEP 70BS is used widely throughout the former USSR by the purchasers of the earlier TEP 70 variety.

Chapter 16

Luxembourg

The national operator is **Société Nationale des Chemins de Fer Luxembourgeois (CFL)**.

Similar to the SNCF Class BB 12000, 20 of the 'Flatiron' CFL Class 3600s were built by Le Matériel de Traction Électrique (MTE) between 1958 and 1959. With a top speed of 75mph and an impressive power output of 3,550hp, the Luxembourg operator found good use for them on local passenger traffic and freight duties before replacement by the Class 4000s. 3614 stands at Luxembourg on a local commuter service in 1990. Two examples of the popular class have been saved for preservation.

CFL received four Nohab locos in 1955, the Class 1600s, to the same design as those used in neighbouring Belgium, the Luxembourg locos being part of the AFB (Anglo-Franco-Belge) order and acquired as part of an agreement with their larger neighbour to provide additional cross-border services. 1604 and SNCB Nohab 5404 are seen during a photo stop at Clervaux, en route from Troisvierges to Liège, on Mercia Charters *Alter Ego* railtour on 16 April 2011. All of the 1600 fleet, except 1601, have been preserved following their withdrawal in the 1990s. 1604 was selected by the Luxembourg Office for Heritage Preservation with 1604 Classics a.s.b.l.

Chapter 17

Macedonia

The national operator is **Makedonski Železnici (MŽ); Македонски Железници (МЖ).**

The Class 661 was built by EMD for Yugoslavian Railways between 1960 and 1972 and has an output of 1,950hp and a top speed of 75mph. Makedonski Železnici (MŽ)/Македонски Железници (МЖ) inherited a number of examples after the break-up of the former Yugoslavia and still use them to this day on passenger duties. On 18 February 2013, 661 234 stands at Kičevo with a train for Skopje. The stock availability and condition in Macedonia leaves much to be desired. Running water is sparse and the steam heating was effective only in the coach nearest the loco. The views, the engine noise and the hospitality made up for the lack of facilities.

Chapter 18

Netherlands

The national operator is **Nederlandse Spoorwegen (NS)**.

Built by Metropolitan-Vickers between 1953 and 1955, the Nederlandse Spoorwegen Class 1500s were originally supplied for British Railways as EM2s (Class 77s) for use on the Woodhead Line between Sheffield and Manchester. With the downgrade of that route to freight only the locos were sold to the Netherlands on their withdrawal in 1969. The whole fleet of seven locos, using the same 1,500V DC supply with an output of 2300hp and a top speed of 90mph, began work on NS shortly after, focussed on the Den Haag to Venlo route. With deliveries of Class 1600s to NS continuing, the EM2 fleet was withdrawn in 1986, though 1501 has been preserved and has featured on a number of railtours. On 16 June 2001, 1501 is seen on a tour at Amersfoort.

Alsthom-Atlantique and MTE Creusot-Loire built 58 of the classic French-designed NS Class 1600/1800s between 1981 and 1983. The 1.5kV DC loco has a design speed of 120mph (though operates at a maximum of 100mph) with an output of 6,200hp. In 1999, the locos in the number range 1638–1658 were allocated to NS-Reizigers for passenger use (forming the 1800 Class), the originally numbered locos being allocated to NS Cargo and retaining their 16xx classification. Ten more locos were transferred to passenger duties in later years. All the 1600/1800s have been given names, and here 1857 *Rotterdam* stands at Amsterdam on 21 August 2010. The Class 1700s are a physically similar, but technically more modernised, type also used on NS.

Chapter 19

Northern Ireland

The national operator is **Northern Ireland Railways (NIR)**.

The NIR Class 111s belong to the General Motors Electro-Motive Division (EMD) JT22CW series of locomotives and bear many similarities to the IE Class 071s. Over the years, the two types have been interchangeable on both sides of the border. NIR has three of the type, 111, 112 and 113, which were delivered in 1980. The fleet is now mainly restricted to engineering duties with their tasks on Enterprise services to Dublin taken over by IE Class 201s and no internal hauled services or freight. Like the 071s they have a 2,250hp EMD 12-645E3C power unit and a top speed of 90mph. On 5 April 2008, 113 pulls into Bangor on a railtour from Dublin.

Chapter 20

Norway

The national operator is **Vygruppen**, branded as **Vy** and formerly the **Norwegian State Railways (NSB)**.

The Di4 Class was built for NSB by Henschel in 1980 and delivered in 1981. Featuring an EMD 16-645E3B power unit rated at 3,290hp and a top speed of 87mph, the five locos were intended to supplement, and eventually replace, the remaining Di3s (Nohabs) still in use on the northern lines. The Di4s are technically related to the MEs supplied to DSB, and also, to a lesser extent, the EI 17 (electric locos) for NSB, also by Henschel and have many advanced features, including three-phase asynchronous traction motors. NSB went on to order Di6s rather than a follow-on for the Di4s. With the return of the Di6s to Germany, Di4s are now the only main-line diesels on NSB's books. On 20 June 2015, Di4 654 waits at Fauske with a Trondheim to Bodø train.

Chapter 21

Poland

The national operator is **Polskie Koleje Państwowe SA (PKP)**.

The EP07s are 3,000V DC electric locomotives and are a modification of the original EU07 Class; 97 of the 483-strong fleet were rebuilt between 1995 and 2003. The rebuilt locomotives had new traction motors and a change in gear ratio to improve performance on passenger services. Nicknamed 'Siódemka' ('the Seven') or 'Anglik' ('the Englishman') they work many regional services throughout the PKP system. The 2,680hp, 78mph locomotives were originally built by Pafawag of Wrocław and Cegielski of Poznan between 1965 and 1994 as a development of the EU06 (itself based on the BR Class 83). On the evening of 3 March 2016, EP07-198 waits at Poznan Glowny on a regional terminating service.

Built by Pafawag between 1986 and 1997, the EP09 was the first high-speed Polish electric locomotive. Nicknamed 'Dziewiątka' ('the Nine') or 'Epoka' ('the Era'), the 3,900hp 3,000V DC locos have a top speed of 100mph. The design of the 47-strong fleet built on the success of earlier types, including the EP07s. After some delayed testing they entered service in 1988, working mostly on the high-speed CMK (Central Rail Line) from Warsaw to Kraków/Katowice and today can be seen on most of the intercity routes from Warsaw. The design evolved during construction and PKP are updating all locos to the same spec as the last two locos completed in 1998. Here, EP09-041 waits at Poznan on a Warsaw service on 4 March 2016.

On 12 February 2012, 370 007 waits at Poznan on an intercity service to Warsaw. In the background 'Woodenlino' EN 57 667 stands with a local stopping train. The PKP Class 370s are part of Siemens' 'Taurus' family of ES64 electric locomotives which are sold throughout Europe. In Poland, the ten locomotives in the class were classified as EU44 from the previous system, have a top speed of 140mph, supply voltages of 15/25kV AC and 1,500/3,000V DC overhead and were introduced between 2008 and 2011.

On 3 March 2016, Su42 504 waits at Krzyz on a regional working to Trzcianka. The Su42, built by Fablok between 1967 and 1972, is a mixed-traffic single-cab Bo-Bo diesel-electric with a top speed of 56mph and a power output of 800hp. The Su42s were originally converted from SM42s in the 1970s by the addition of ETH capability. Later, 40 Su42s (classified as Su42-5xx) were converted from SP42s between 1999 and 2000, again with ETH being added, though these later loco rebuilds have a separate Caterpillar diesel power unit for train heating generation. The type has a very wide range of nicknames from 'Zebra', 'Fablok' (after the builder), 'Polsat' (from the livery, similar to a Polish TV Channel) to 'Wibrator' (due to excessive engine tremors).

The SU45 is PKP's standard mixed-traffic diesel-electric loco. Built by Cegielski in Wrocław between 1970 and 1976, the 102t Co-Co has a 1,750hp power unit (derived from a Fiat design) and a top speed of 75mph. Originally fitted with boilers (and designated Class SP45), 191 of the original 268 locos were converted to ETH supply between 1987 and 1998. They are nicknamed 'Fiat', or 'Suka' ('Bitch') from the first two letters of the Class type. On 3 March 2016, SU45-079 waits at Trzcianka with an EN7 EMU in attendance.

At the closed station of Lipiny Odrzańskie on the line from Nowa Sol to Wolsztyn, on a railtour from Berlin to an open day at the Polish Steam Centre at Wolsztyn, Ok1-359 and Ok22-31 perform a run past on 29 August 1992. The PKP 4-6-0 Class OK1 was the Polish designation for the classic Prussian P8 type used widely throughout Europe and produced between 1908 and 1928. The type became Poland's most common passenger steam loco class. Poland received 192 P8s after the First World War as reparations and another 65 were ordered and imported in 1922 and 1923. After being recaptured by the Germans in the Second World War (with some taken by the Soviets), after the end of the war Poland again received OK1s as reparations. There were 429 this time, numbered Ok1-1 to 429. The fleet lasted in service until 1981. Ok1-359 has been preserved at Wolsztyn. Under PKP Classification 'O' stands for mixed traffic, k for 4-6-0 and the 1 is in the 1−10 range for locos of Prussian or German origin. The Ok22 was a 4-6-0 passenger loco based on the Prussian P8s (PKP Class OK1s), 190 of which were built for PKP by Hanomag (of Germany; they built the first 5 locos) and Fablok between 1923 and 1934. The class bore many similarities with the Ty23.

The Ol49 class is a standard ('O') mixed-traffic 2-6-2 steam ('l') loco with a rated output of 1,300hp and a top speed of 62mph. Between 1951 and 1954, 116 of the class were built by Fablok of Chrzanów, Poland; 112 for PKP and four for North Korea. The Ol49s replaced older Prussian Ok1 and Ok22 types on PKP. Two examples of the class are still in active use out of Wolsztyn (Ol49 59 and Ol49 69) though the heritage steam operations there are due to end in 2020. With the air temperature hovering around 18°C, Ol49-59 waits at Wolsztyn with a return service to Poznan Glowny on 11 February 2012.

Chapter 22

Portugal

The national operator is **Comboios de Portugal, EPE (CP)**.

CP's 2500 Class electrics were its first electric locos. The locomotives, built by a consortium, termed Groupement d'Etude d'Electrification Monophase 50Hz, comprising Henschel, Alsthom and Sorefame, were introduced between 1956 and 1957 for the newly electrified line north from Lisbon in the 1950s. However, with a rated output of 2,790hp and a maximum speed of only 75mph, the locomotives were quickly superseded by later designs and were all withdrawn by 2009, with one preserved. The locos were used on some regional passenger duties in later years, as shown here on 13 April 1993 at Alfareios on IR811, the 08.05 Lisbon SA to Guarda.

The Alsthom 2601 Class, similar to the SNCF's BB 15000 series, were the staple motive power for Lisbon–Porto services and also on the Sud Express (train 313, the 09.30 Paris Austerlitz–Lisbon). The locos, nicknamed 'Nez Cassée' ('Broken Nose'), were also similar to the NS Class 1600s. Nine later locos, the Class 2620s, were assembled in Portugal by Sorefame in 1987.The Portuguese locos were all withdrawn by 2013 though five may be revived under expansion plans put in place by CP. 2605 is seen here on the service from Paris at Pampilhosa on 9 April 1993.

Built by Brissonneau & Lotz and Sorefame between 1961 and 1964, CP's Class 1200s are the same loco type (BB 63000) used by the SNCF. However, in Portugal this type is tasked with local passenger and freight workings. The 25 Portuguese locos were 825hp diesel-electrics with a top speed of 50mph. In contrast to the SNCF BB 63000 Class of the same design (used in France almost exclusively for shunting), the 1200s, nicknamed 'Lawnmowers' by some European enthusiasts, were possibly just about powerful enough in pairs for local workings loaded to three coaches, as shown here at Tunes. Some of the CP locos were sold to Argentina in 2007. Plans to revive some of the 1200 Class for shunting were cancelled recently in favour of reviving additional numbers of the more powerful and more reliable Class 1400 fleet. On 12 April 1993, 'Sewing Machine' 1200 Class 1289 waits at Tunes with a three-coach local working.

Between 1967 and 1969, 67 of the Class 1400 diesel-electric Bo-Bos were built for CP. Like the BR Class 20s they were based on the locos built by English Electric (initially, and later by Sorefame under licence) and proved to be highly reliable. They have also proved highly popular with British and Portuguese enthusiasts. They are fitted with an English Electric 8CSVT power unit that is essentially a half-size version of the one in the Class 50 and give an output of 1,330hp. With a top speed of 65mph, the locos are a true mixed-traffic design and are still in use today on freight and passenger work around Portugal. During the winter of 2018/19, Douro Valley electrification blockade CP Class 1400 1413 arrives at Rede, working the 11.05 Marco de Canaveses to Pocinho service on 21 February 2019. The beautiful steep-sided vineyard scenery of the Douro Valley can be seen to good effect at this crossover station on the largely single-track line.

With a mixture of Budd and Schindler stock, two unidentified CP Class 1400s approach Livracao on the Douro Valley line on a service from Regua to Porto Sao Bento on 14 April 1993. The same stock and locomotives are still in use today on the Douro Valley line.

In the last few days of the Douro blockade, 1455 leaves Ermida on 29 March 2019 on the 11.05 Marco de Canaveses to Pocinho. This photo was taken with a long lens from a main highway bridge, only later did the author find out that pedestrians were banned from it.

The Alco 1501/1521 classes were brought in as early as 1948 with the introduction of the second series being completed in 1951. Funded by Marshall Plan aid, the 1501 class were some of the first main-line diesel locos in use in Europe and, despite limited dedicated diesel servicing facilities, proved highly reliable. The RSC-2 type was exported to a number of countries and also saw use in the USA, generally as a yard shunter. With an A1A-A1A wheel arrangement and an impressive output of 2,000hp, the locos remained in use with CP until the year 2000 with some still seeing occasional use with private operators. One example is preserved at Portugal's National Railway Museum at Entroncamento. The locos had a top speed of 75mph but in later years were restricted to local passenger duties such as this appearance by 1512 on 12 April 1993 on train 17224, the 14.50 Praias Sado to Barreiro local service.

The CP Class 1550s were 2,000hp V12 251C power unit-powered 75mph C-C locomotives built by MLW of Canada. The type was designated MX 620 by the manufacturers, and between 1973 and 1980, 145 examples were supplied to a range of countries, including Sri Lanka, Tunisia, Greece, Cameroon and Brazil. The type was also produced under licence by Spanish manufacturers CAF. The first of the 19 Portuguese locos entered service in 1973. 1554 stands at Figueira da Foz after arrival on train IC501, the 17.30 from Lisbon, on a very rainy 12 April 1993. The CP fleet was withdrawn in 2012.

The ten Class 1800s were built by English Electric in 1968. They were based on the BR Class 50 design with an English Electric 2,700hp 16 CSVT engine. This type shared many components with the Class 1400s, which were also built by EE. With their top speed of 87mph, they were traditionally used on Barreiro (Lisbon) to Faro (the Algarve) express services and proved popular with both British and indigenous enthusiasts. The class was displaced when the Algarve line was electrified, and the fleet was withdrawn in 2001. All of the fleet has been cut up bar one loco, 1805, which has been saved as part of the CP Railway Museum collection and has been repainted into the original blue livery. There are many plans to return this loco to main-line use, and it was booked for a tour in May 2016, but efforts to revive it have so far come to naught. A pair of 50s (or at least, CP Class 1800s) are shown here on a timetabled passenger train in Portugal. 1802 and an unidentified class member wait at Barreiro (the southern port terminus of the railway from the Algarve to the Portuguese capital of Lisbon) on a train to Faro on 11 April 1993.

On 10 April 1993, CP Class 50 variant 1810 leaves Tunes on IR872, the 15.45 Vila Real to Barreiro service.

French manufacturer Alstom and Portuguese company SOREFAME built 13 Class 1900s for CP. The SACM power unit generated 3,300hp and the type was based on the SNCF 72000s but were unsilenced. This deafening class of locos predominantly worked freight for CP but occasionally substituted for Class 1800s, as 1902 is doing here at Barreiro on IC573, the 18.13 service to Villa Real, on 11 April 1993. Physically similar to the French locos, the Portuguese 1900s were built under licence by Sorefame. The later 1930 Class have a higher top speed of 75mph and 17 were built in 1981 for use on passenger services. They saw use on the Algarve services but were withdrawn in 2018.

The 1960 Class 'Thumpers' were built by Bombardier MLW from 1979 to 1980. Thirteen of the 3,000hp locos were introduced and they had a top speed of 75mph. They were used mainly on freight, particularly on the Beria Alta Line, where they were also booked to work the heavy Sud Express overnight service from Paris Austerlitz to Lisbon Santa Appollonia. 1964 is seen here at Pampilhosa on 9 April 1993. Two of the fleet remain in service, exclusively on freight duties, though they are likely to be withdrawn in the next two years.

The Alsthom Serie 9020 were metre-gauge diesel-electrics built for CP and introduced in 1976. The locos, with a top speed of 43mph and an impressively high power output of 1,050hp from their SACM power units, gave reliable service on the isolated narrow-gauge lines in the north of the country. Closure of most of the Portuguese narrow-gauge network in the early noughties saw the fleet withdrawn, though some of the locos were sold to Madarail of Madagascar. On 14 April 1993, Alstom metre-gauge diesel 9030 arrives at Mirandela on train 6205, the 11.21 from Tua. The 23.5-mile-long line closed in 2008.

Chapter 23

Romania

The national operator is **Căile Ferate Române (CFR)**.

With an output of 8,900hp and a top speed of 100mph, the Class 47 electrics are the most powerful locomotives in service with CFR. There are two subtypes, the freight Class 474s and the passenger Class 477s. The locomotives are updated and refurbished versions of the standard CFR Class 40 and 41s, rebuilt by Softronic of Craiova (477s) and PROMAT (474s) between 2006 and the current day. Over 100 Class 47s are now in service. Some locos have also been converted for Hungarian operator MMV. On 26 February 2020, 477 551 leaves Sighisoara on a Cluj Napoca to Brasov train.

The Class 60 and Class 62 diesel-electrics are a distinctive Romanian Electroputere design, which was originally developed by SLM/Sulzer/Brown Boveri and built between 1959 and 1981; style-wise, they were based on a Swiss loco (the electric AE 6/6). They both feature Sulzer 2,100hp power units with the Class 60s having a top speed of 62mph and the Class 62s, 75mph. Around 60 Class 60s and 20 Class 62s remain in service with CFR. The design was also exported, becoming the Polish ST43, the Bulgarian Class 06 and the Chinese ND2/3; over 2,500 examples were built. More recently, some have found use with private freight operators in Spain, Germany and Italy. On 24 February 2020, 62 114 stands at Podu Olt with the 16.05 Sibiu to Craiova service.

Previously designated as Class 65, the CFR Class 64, together with the Class 66, is now the standard Romanian passenger diesel loco type for higher-speed services. Rebuilt by Electroputere with a 2,130hp EMD V8 8-710G power unit, the type is essentially a modernised version of the Class 60 with a new bodyshell and GM power plant. Fifty examples were constructed from 2004. The ten Class 66s are a 75mph variant. On 24 February 2020, with the splendid vista of the snow-capped Carpathian Mountains as a background, 64 117 arrives at Sibiu with train IR 1623, the 09.55 from Bucharest Gara de Nord.

The Electroputere LE 5100 family (or Class EA0) of electric locos are designated as Classes 40, 41 and 42 by CFR and are a type developed by ASEA, with the bulk of production being carried out by the Romanian manufacturer. The locos, similar to Norway's El.15s, originally numbered 933 examples, though many are now stored out of use. The top speed is 75mph for the 40s, 100mph for the 41s and 120mph for the high-speed test locos of Class 42. All of the family has a power output of 6,800hp. 40 077 stands at Brasov on a service from Bucharest Gara de Nord on 26 February 2020.

Chapter 24

Serbia

The national operator is **Železnice Srbije (ŽS); Железнице Србије**.

The Class 444s, nicknamed 'Severina', were built between 2004 and 2007 for Serbian Railways (Železnice Srbije) by Mašinska of Niš who upgraded 30 of the Class 441 locos with thyristor control. With a top speed of 62, 75, 87 or 99mph, the locomotives have not been fully utilised on Serbia's run-down railway network. On 22 February 2013, 444 007 stands at Belgrade on an international service to Zagreb that travelled at a maximum of 30mph, taking nine hours to travel to the Croatian capital.

Chapter 25

Slovakia

The national operator is **Železničná spoločnosť (ZSSK)**.

350 016 stands at Brno in 1990. The Class 350s were introduced by Škoda in 1974 as dual-voltage 3,000V DC and 25kV AC express passenger locos with a maximum speed of 100mph. They are a development of Classes 150/151 and on partition all 20 locos went to Slovakia. With 5,400hp available and a top speed of 100mph, they have been nicknamed 'Gorilla' due to their impressive performance. They have been replaced by the new Škoda Class 380s on much of Slovakia's prestige passenger work.

Chapter 26

Slovenia

The national operator is **Slovenske železnice (SŽ)**.

Twenty-five of the Class 644s (of the standard EMD G22U type) were assembled for Jugoslavenske željeznice between 1973 and 1974 by MACOSA of Spain. After the break-up of Yugoslavia, all of the fleet was inherited by Slovenia, though some examples were later sold on to Serbia and Macedonia. The locomotives have a power output of 1,660hp and a top speed of 50mph. SŽ operates a car train (Avtovlak) through the Bohinj tunnel connecting Bohinjska Bistrica with Podbrdo, Most na Soči and Nova Gorica. The service is the only remaining booked diesel-hauled passenger service in Slovenia and motive power is generally provided by 644 020. Here, the familiar locomotive is seen at Most na Soči on the Avtovlak to Bohinjska Bistrica on 25 February 2014.

Forty Class 342s were supplied to the former Yugoslavia by Italian supplier Ansaldo (now Hitachi Rail Italy) between 1968 and 1970. The locos, nicknamed 'Mofa' or occasionally 'Mopeds' because of their perceived poor performance (they only have 2,400hp on tap), have been used exclusively in Slovenia due to their Italian-standard 3,000V DC supply. Only a handful of the 75mph locos remain in use, working throughout Slovenia on intercity, local and regional work. Fourteen of the Class 342s were sold to Italian operators FNM and FER in the noughties. SŽ 342 014 is seen at Ljubljana on a train to Rijeka on 14 February 2012.

The SŽ Class 363 is a 3kV DC electric built between 1975 and 1977 by Alsthom. A member of the 'Nez Cassé' ('Broken Nose') family, together with SNCF Class 6500s and NS Class 1600s, 39 locos were supplied to Yugoslavia, all having been inherited by Slovenian Railways (Slovenske železnice). When built they were designed to receive the Italian standard 3000V DC supply. In Slovenia they are nicknamed 'Brižita' ('Brigitte') after Brigitte Bardot (a common name for many locomotive classes with protruding cab fronts). With an output of 3,980hp and a top speed of 78mph, the fleet is gradually being replaced on most duties by the Siemens-built 'Taurus' locomotives but do occasionally appear on top link passenger duties and as replacements for the Class 342 'Mopeds' on local and regional work. 363 002 is seen in charge of the daily Budapest to Ljubljana service in 2010.

Chapter 27
Spain

The national operator is **Renfe Operadora (RENFE)**.

On 16 April 1993, RENFE Class 289 Bo-Bo 289 034 waits at Medina del Campo on the Sud Express train 310, the 15.10 Lisbon–Paris Austerlitz. Introduced in 1969, the Mitsubishi design was built under licence by Construcciones y Auxiliar de Ferrocarriles. The 4,200hp locos had a top speed of 50/81mph and operated on 1,500 and 3,000V DC. The Japanese-designed loco worked the train as far as the French border at Hendaye, where the bogies were changed from Iberian to standard gauge for the journey onwards. Many of the fleet were converted into dual units for freight work and designated Class 289.1.

Chapter 28

Sweden

The national operator is **Statens Järnvägar (SJ)**.

The Swedish loco manufacturer ASEA (Allmänna Svenska Elektriska Aktiebolaget), now part of ABB/Bombardier after an initial merger with Brown Boveri, had great success in producing and exporting electric locomotives in the Rc family. The locos, first introduced in 1967, use thyristor control, which replaced the diode control of the earlier types. There have been eight separate loco types in the range used in Sweden, including the freight-only Rm Class and various Rc subtypes. These subtypes are generally defined by their top speed; Rc1–Rc5 have a top speed of 84mph while Rc3 and Rc6 have a top speed of 100mph and the Rc7s were 112mph converts for high-speed vice duty (when the X2000 EMUs were unavailable) though inadequate braking systems saw them revert to Rc6s. In terms of output each class has a continuous rating of 4,800hp. Other buyers of the Rc type included: Austria (ÖBB) which had ten Class 1043 locos; Iran (RAI) with eight Class 40–700 locos; Norway (NSB) with 17 Class El 16 locos; and the USA (Amtrak, SEPTA, MARC) with 65 Class AEM-7 locos.

On 22 June 2014, SJ 1326 waits at Narvik (Norway) with the overnight service to Stockholm. The line to Narvik was intended primarily for Swedish iron ore traffic from Kiruna (Narvik being one of the world's most northerly ice-free ports), though a limited passenger service is in use.

Chapter 29

Switzerland

The national operators are:

German – **Schweizerische Bundesbahnen (SBB)**.
French – **Chemins de fer Fédéraux Suisses (CFF)**.
Italian – **Ferrovie Federali Svizzere (FFS)**.

The GE 4/4s are metre-gauge Bo-Bo electrics operated by the Rhaetian Railway, otherwise known as the Rhatische Bahn, or RhB, situated in the south-east corner of Switzerland in the canton of Graubunden. Ten of the locos were built by SLM, BBC and MFO between 1947 and 1954 and later rebuilt between 1986 and 1991. Operating on the RhB's 11kV and 16⅔Hz overhead AC supply, they have a power output of 1,590hp and a top speed of 50mph. On 15 February 2004, 605 and 606 stand at Arosa on a relief ski special train for Chur. Four of the class remain in service with two earmarked for preservation.

The RhB Ge 4/4^{II} Class were built by SLM and BBC between 1973 and 1984 with 23 locos being produced. They went on to become the RhB's main mixed-traffic locos. They have a top speed of 56mph and an output of 2,210hp. Twenty-three of the locos were delivered, numbered 61–633. The fleet was rebuilt in 2004 and the locos largely remain in service. One loco, number 611, is earmarked for preservation. On 22 November 2003, 625 stands at Chur with an empty stock working.

The 12 locomotives in the RhB Ge 4/4^{III} Class were built by SLM/ABB and Adtranz between 1993 and 1999. With a top speed of 62mph and an output of 4,160hp, they are the most powerful narrow-gauge electric locomotives in the world. The class now haul most services on the Albula line to St. Moritz. All locomotives in the class feature advertising liveries. 651 is seen here arriving at Preda on 16 February 2004 on a Chur to St. Moritz service.

The RhB Ge 6/6ʺ Class articulated metre-gauge Bo-Bo-Bo locos of the Rhaetian Railway were introduced in 1958 with two prototypes, followed by seven production locos in 1965. Built by BBC, SLM and MFO, they were originally delivered in green; the distinctive RhB red livery was applied in 1985. The Ge 6/6ʺs have a top speed of 50mph and a maximum output of 2,400hp. They were originally used to haul heavy express services over the Albula line but today are mostly used on freight traffic. Here, 704 stands at Chur on a train from Davos on 22 November 2003.

The Matterhorn Gotthard Bahn was formed in 2003 from the merger of the Brig-Visp-Zermatt and Furka-Oberalp railways. Here, Class HGe 4/4ʺ Number 3 *Dom* (an ex-BVZ loco) stands at Furka awaiting departure on 22 November 2003. The HGe 4/4ʺ was built by SLM between 1986 and 1990 with electrical equipment from BBC/ABB. With a maximum speed of 56mph (22mph on rack) and power output of 2,600hp, the type has proven very reliable in service. Thirteen of the locos were introduced for use on Glacier Express services between Zermatt and Disentis-Muster via Brig and Andermatt.

Chapter 30
Turkey

The national operator is **Türkiye Cumhuriyeti Devlet Demiryolları (TCDD)**.

Eighty-six of the DE22000s were built in Turkey by Tülomsaş, under licence from General Motors Electro-Motive Diesel (EMD), between 1985 and 1989. With an installed GM 16 645E power unit, an output of 2200hp and a top speed of 75mph, the Turkish locos are based on the EMD G26CW-2 design (the export version of the SD40-2) and were also supplied to Australia, Croatia (Class 2062), Indonesia, Iran, Israel, Morocco and Hong Kong using the highly successful 645 power unit. The DE22s are used as mixed-traffic locos by TCDD in Turkey though most of their duties are on freight with some overnight sleeper traffic and long-distance passenger services. Here, DE 22 062 leaves Ankara on the empty stock of an overnight service from Adana on 29 October 2013.

Introduced in 1970 to replace the remaining steam locos in Turkey, the DE24000s were assembled under licence from Matériel de Traction Électrique (MTE), a forerunner of Alstom, until 1984; there was an eventual total of 418 locos in the fleet. The Pielstick 16PA4-powered diesel-electrics have an output of 2360hp and a top speed of 75mph and were already proven in the SNCF 67300s. On 26 October 2013, DE 24 376 is seen at Balikesir on a train to Izmir.

The DE33000s were introduced as a development of the DE22000s in 2003 by Tülomsaş, and between then and 2004, 89 locos were built under licence. They share many parts with the DE22000s but have an uprated 3,300hp power unit, through use of a large turbocharger, and a top speed of 80mph. The class is mostly used on freight duties but has appeared on some sleeper services, as shown here where DE 33 042 is at Konya on the 19.15 overnight to Izmir on 29 October 2013.

Chapter 31

USA

Intercity services are provided by **Amtrak**.

Amtrak looked to replace its F40s in the 1990s with a lighter and more powerful loco. General Electric supplied 46 of the Genesis Dash 8-40BPs as well as 18 dual-mode P32AC-DMs, able to run into New York Penn Station, and 208 of the uprated 4,200hp P42DCs for Amtrak and 21 for VIA Rail for wider use on long-distance traffic. Members of the Genesis family still provide the backbone for intercity passenger haulage in the US and Canada up to the present day. Genesis superpower is on display at Portland with 817 and an unidentified fellow class member top and tail on two streamliner coaches on 24 June 2014. Originally turned out in red, white and blue livery for Amtrak, the Genesis locos now feature the standard blue-hooded silver livery as seen here.

The AEM7 Class, known as 'Swedish Meatballs' or 'Toasters' (due to their striated bodysides, designed by Budd) were built by EMD and based on a Swedish design. They had a top speed of 125mph and an output of 7,000hp. In addition to Amtrak, the class was used on Maryland services (between Baltimore and Washington) and on Penn Transport trains out of Philadelphia. On 25 June 2014, AEM7 914 stands at the buffers at Boston on a service from Washington.

EMD's GP (General Purpose) series of locomotives, often referred to as 'Geeps', gave much better bi-directional visibility than the company's single-cabbed F-Units. Side access doors also gave much better maintenance access and the GP design proved to be very influential towards future North American loco design. The GPs ranged from the 1,500hp GP7s right up to the 3,000hp GP40s, 1243 of which were produced between 1965 and 1971. The GP 40MCs for MBTA were originally GP40-2LWs, supplied to Canadian National between 1973 and 1975 and rebuilt by AMF between 1997 and 1998. 1115 is seen here at Boston North on an MBTA service to Lowell on 23 June 2014.

The F40 PH Class was a very successful EMD product. Initially ordered in numbers by Amtrak in 1976 and later by Via Rail (Canada) and many commuter operators, the loco became the most widespread passenger locomotive in North America. As 3,000 or 3,200hp Bo-Bos they have a top speed of 103 or 110mph. Since the end of the 1990s, the type has been relegated to more secondary duties such as the one undertaken here by F40PH-2C 1050, which is on an MBTA service from Boston to Salem and is shown at its infamous destination on 23 June 2014.

141 of the GE Dash 8-40B Class were built between 1988 and 1989. The 4,000hp (an astoundingly high output for a four-axle loco) freight type is related to the GE Genesis series locos used by Amtrak and a number of Suburban operators. On 29 June 2014, 8524 stands at Saratoga Springs after working a service in from North Creek. The Saratoga and North Creek Railway began operations in July 2011 in the Upper Hudson River area of the Adirondack Mountains in New York State. However, poor patronage saw the line close to passengers and freight in 2018, though there are plans to reopen it.

On 23 October 2018, Long Island Railroad Class DE30AC 412 leaves Northport on a service from Port Jefferson to Jamaica. The 24 DE30AC (diesel-only) locos are physically very similar to the company's 21 DM30AC (dual-power) sister locomotives. The locos were built in 1999 by GM to replace older locos including F-Units, GP38s and Alco FA1s and FA2s. The EMD locos have a top speed of 100mph on diesel and 80mph on electric (third rail pick up) and an EMD 12N-710G3B-EC 3,000hp power unit. The locos are still in service and power many of the longer-distance LIRR services on the island and to and from Manhattan (Penn Station). The LIRR, part of New York's Metropolitan Transportation Authority (MTA), is America's busiest commuter railway, though the DE30s also see plenty of use on non-peak services, as shown here.

On 30 June 2014, Long Island Railroad dual-power single-cab diesel-electric Class DM30AC 502 arrives at Jamaica on a train from Montauk. The locos are very similar to the diesel-only DE30ACs and were also built in 1999 by GM to replace the company's older F-Units, GP38s and Alco FA1s and FA2s. They have a top speed of 100mph on diesel (with an EMD 12N-710G3B power unit) and 80mph on third rail electric supply. The services from Montauk pass through the Hamptons on their way to Manhattan (Penn Station) though most commuters from these areas travel by car rather than railroad.

The complexity of US loco classification and numbering is ably demonstrated by the history of locomotive 4100. EMD built a wide range of variants of their popular GP40 Bo-Bos, including the 13 GP40Ps supplied to the Central Railroad of New Jersey (CNJ) in 1968. After their boilers were replaced with ETH generators, they were reclassified as GP40PH in the early 1980s. They were finally rebuilt as GP40PH-2s in 1991and 1992. On 21 June 2014, 'Class Leader' 4100, 'on the point' of a New Jersey Transit service from Secaucus, departs from Wood Ridge on a Bergen County line train from Secaucus to Suffern. This loco was previously owned by the CNJ and numbered GP40P 3681. 4100 and 4101 remain in service but the rest of the fleet has been converted back to non-revenue earning GP40-2s and/or replaced by ALP-45DPs.

Manufacturer List

Manufacturer	City	Country	Classes of loco(s) featured	History/Notes
23rd August Locomotive Works (MALAXA)	Bucharest	Romania	DR Class 119, MÁV M47	Originally FAUR, renamed FAUR in 1990 and privatised; now part of Bega Group.
50 Hz Traction Union (ASEA, ELIN [de], SAAS Sécheron, SGP/Simmering-Graz-Pauker)	Various	Various	JŽ Class 441	
ABB Trazione	Vado Ligure	Italy	E464	Taken over by ADTranz, then Bombardier.
ACEC (Ateliers de Construction Électriques de Charleroi)	Charleroi	Belgium	MÁV V43, SNCB Class 16, 26, 62	Bought by Alsthom in 1989.
Adtranz	Berlin	Germany	RhB Ge 4/4III Class, DB Class 146	A merger in 1996 of Daimler-Benz and ABB; bought by Bombardier in 2001.
AEG (Allgemeine Elektrizitäts-Gesellschaft AG)	Frankfurt am Main	Germany	DB Class 103, 11, 140, 150 and MÁV V43	Bought by ABB, then Adtranz; now owned by Bombardier.
Alco (American Locomotive Company)	Schenectady, New York	USA	CP 1501 Class	Licences for locomotives were transferred to MLW in 1969.
Alstom	Saint-Ouen-sur-Seine	France	NS 1800, SNCB Class 18, SNCF BB 17000, 22200 and 7200, CP 2500, 2601 and 9020,	Originally Alsthom; multinational global company.
AnsaldoBreda S.p.A.	Naples	Italy	HŽ Class 1061	Now Hitachi Rail Italy.
Arnold Jung Lokomotivfabrik	Kirchen, Rheinland-Pfalz	Germany	DR Class 41	Stopped loco production in 1976.
ASEA (Allmänna Svenska Elektriska Aktiebolaget)	Västerås	Sweden	SJ Rc Class	Now part of ABB/Bombardier after initial merger with Brown Boveri.

Manufacturer	City	Country	Classes of loco(s) featured	History/Notes
Batignolles-Châtillon	Paris	France	DR Class 41	Now Spie-Batignolles.
Berliner Maschinenbau/BMAG – Schwartzkopff	Berlin	Germany	DR 41, 44, 50, 99.73-76 Class, PKP Ok1	Operated as Berliner Maschinenbau-Actien-Gesellschaft vormals L. Schwartzkopff, Berlin.
BN Constructions Ferroviaires et Métalliques	Bruges	Berlin	SNCB Class 16, 26, 62	Formerly La Brugeoise et Nivelles; bought by Bombardier in 1988.
Bombardier	Berlin (HQ)	Germany	CP Class 1960, DB Class 185, AMT ALP-45DP	Multinational Canadian company.
Borsig	Berlin	Germany	DR Class 41, 44, 50	Still active today.
Brissonneau & Lotz	Nantes	France	CP Class 1200, SNCF 67400	Absorbed into Alsthom in 1972.
Brown Boveri & Cie (BBC)	Baden	Switzerland	DB Class 103, 111 and 140, MÁV V43, RhB GE 4/4 and 4/4^{II} and Ge 6/6^{II}	Merged with ASEA in January 1988 to form the ABB group.
Canadian Locomotive Company (CLC)	Kingston, Ontario	Canada	SNCB Class 29	Became Whitcomb-Baldwin in 1948; bankrupt and closed in 1969.
Cegielski	Poznan	Poland	PKP SU45	Still operating; state owned.
ČKD (Českomoravská Kolben-Daněk)	Prague	Czech Republic	ČD 720, 742, 749, 753, 770	Renamed ČKD Tatra then bought by Siemens in 2001.
Cockerill	Seraing	Belgium	SNCB Class 51	Wideranging engineering company.
Compagnie Électro-Mécanique (CEM)	Paris	France	SNCF 66400	Subsidiary company of Brown, Boveri & Cie; bought by Alsthom in 1983.
Construcciones y Auxiliar de Ferrocarriles (CAF)	Beasain	Spain	RENFE Class 289	'Construction & Other Railway Services'; includes CAF USA and CAF UK.
Đuro Đaković Grupa d.d.	Slavonski Brod	Croatia	JŽ Class 441	Still active.
Electroputere	Craiova	Romania	CFR Class 40, 41, 62, 64	Ceased railway work in 2019.
English Electric	Newton-Le-Willows	England	CP 1400, CP 1800	Merged with GEC in 1969; this merged with Alsthom in 1989.
Fablok (Fabryka Lokomotyw)	Chrzanów	Poland	PKP Ok22, OL49, Su42	Ceased trading in 2013.
Fiat Ferroviaria	Turin	Italy	FS D.445	Bought by Alstom in 2000.

Fives-Lille	Lille	France	SNCF 66400 Class	Now part of The Fives Engineering Group.
Ganz-MÁVAG	Budapest	Hungary	MÁV V43	Now part of AnsaldoBreda.
General Electric	Chicago	USA	Amtrak Genesis Dash 8-40BP, SNCR Dash 8-40B	Sold to Wabtec in 2019.
General Motors Electro-Motive Diesel (EMD)	La Grange, Illinois	USA	IE Classes 071, 181, NIR Class 111, Amtrak AEM7, MBTA GP40 and F40, LIRR DE30AC, AMT F59PH and F59PHI, NJT GP40, MŽ Class 661, HŽ Class 2062, 2063	Since 2010, owned by Caterpillar subsidiary Progress Rail Services.
Groupement d'Etude d'Electrification Monophase 50Hz	Various	Various	CP 2500 Class	Group including Henschel, Alsthom and Sorefame.
Hanomag (Hannoversche Maschinenbau AG)	Hannover	Germany	PKP Ok22	Bought by Komatsu in 1989.
Henschel	Kassel	Germany	DSB Class ME, DB Class 103, 111, 150, 218, CP 2500, BDŽ Class 75, NSB Di4.	Merged in 1976 as Thyssen-Henschel, then in 1990 became ABB Henschel AG. In 1996 was ABB/Adtranz, then Bombardier in 2002.
Kolomna Locomotive Works (Kolomensky Zavod)	Kolomna, Moscow	Russia	LG TEP 70, TEP 70 BS	State owned and still active.
Končar Group	Zagreb	Croatia	HŽ Class 1142, ŽRS and ŽFBH Class 1141	Still active.
Krauss-Maffei	Munich	Germany	DB Class 103, 11, 140, 150, 218, V200, ÖBB 1099	Now part of Siemens AG.
Krupp	Essen	Germany	DB Class 103, 111, 140, 150, 218	Became ThyssenKrupp after merger.
Le Matériel de Traction Électrique (MTE)	Various	France	CFL Class 3600, SNCF BB 7200, NS Class 1800	50/50 subsidiary of Jeumont-Schneider and Creusot-Loire; became Francorail then part of Alsthom in 1987.
Like Hoffmann	Breslau	Germany	PKP Ok1	Absorbed by Alstom in 2009.
LOFAG (Lokomotivfabrik Florisdorf)	Vienna	Austria	DR Class 41	Merged with Simmering-Graz-Pauker in 1958.

Manufacturer	City	Country	Classes of loco(s) featured	History/Notes
MACOSA (Material y Construcciones S.A.)	Valencia, Barcelona	Spain	SŽ Class 644	Sold to GEC Alston in 1989, then Vossloh, now Stadler.
Maschinenbau Kiel (Mak)	Kiel	Germany	DB Class 211, 212, 213, 218 290, V200, NSB DE2700	Bought by Vossloh in 1998.
Maschinenfabrik Esslingen (ME)	Schönefeld	Germany	DR Class 41	Bought by Daimler-Benz in 1965.
Mašinska Industrija Niš	Niš	Serbia	ŽS Class 444	Closed, bankrupt in 2015.
Metropolitan-Vickers	Manchester	England	NS Class 1500	Merged with BTH in 1928 (under AEI Group); bought by GEC in 1967; sold to Marconi in 1999.
MFO (Maschinenfabrik Oerlikon)	Oerlikon	Switzerland	RhB GE 4/4, RhB Ge 6/6^{II}	Taken over by Brown, Boveri & Cie in 1967; in 1988 merged with ASEA to form ABB Group.
MIN Mašinska industrija Niš (МИН Машинска индустрија Ниш)	Niš	Serbia	JŽ Class 441	Closed, bankrupt in 2015.
Mitsubishi	Tokyo	Japan	RENFE Class 289	Still active.
MLW (Montreal Locomotive Works)	Montreal, Quebec	Canada	CP Class 1550, 1960	Formerly part of Alco; taken over by Bombardier, then GE, before closure.
MotivePower (MPI)	Boise, Idaho	USA	GO MP40PH-3C	Originally MK Rail in 1972 (Morrison-Knudsen); merged with Westinghouse in 1999 to form Wabtec.
Nydqvist & Holm AB (NOHAB)	Trollhättan	Sweden	SNCB Class 52, MÁV M61, NSB Di3 (Kosovo)	Closed, bankrupt in 1979.
Officine di Casaralta	Bologna	Italy	FS Class E656	Incorporated by merger into the Firema Trasporti group in 1993.
Officine Meccaniche Reggiane SpA	Reggio Emilia	Italy	FS Class E656	Taken over by Fantuzzi (Fantuzzi Reggiane) and then the American company, Terex Corporation.
October Revolution Locomotive Factory/Voroshilovgrad Locomotive Works	Luhansk	Ukraine	DR Class 132, 142, MÁV M62, BDŽ 07	Now Luhanskteplovoz (Луганськтепловоз or Luhansk Locomotive works).

Manufacturer	City	Country	Class	Notes
Orenstein and Koppel (O&K)	Berlin	Germany	DR Class 41	Left the railway business in 1981.
Pafawag (Państwowa Fabryka Wagonów)	Wrocław	Poland	PKP EP07, EP09	Sold to Bombardier via Adtranz.
SAAS (Société Anonyme des Ateliers de Sécheron)	Geneva	Switzerland	JŽ Class 441	Became ABB in 1989.
Sächsische Maschinenfabrik	Chemnitz, Saxony	Germany	DR 99.73-76 Class	Closed on bankruptcy in 1930.
SACM (Société Alsacienne de Constructions Mécaniques)	Mulhouse, Alsace	France	SNCF 66400	The Alsatian Corporation of Mechanical Engineering.
Schichau-Werke	Elbing	Germany	DR Class 41	Elbing is now in Poland; moved to Bremerhaven in 1945; closed 2009.
Siemens	Munich	Germany	SNCB Class 18, ÖBB 1063, DB Class 103, 111, 140, MÁV V43, NSB DE2700, ÖBB Class 1216, PKP 370	Now Siemens AG.
Siemens Shuckert	Berlin	Germany	ÖBB Class 1099	Absorbed into Siemenns AG in 1966.
Simmering-Graz-Pauker	Vienna	Austria	ÖBB Class 2095	Bought by Siemens 1989.
Škoda	Pilsen	Czech Republic	Class 163, 230, 350	Bought in 2018 by PPF (Finance Group) of the Netherlands.
SLM (Schweizerische Lokomotiv- und Maschinenfabrik)	Winterthur	Switzerland	RhB Ge 4/4^{I}, 4/4^{II} and 4/4^{III}, RhB Ge 6/6^{II}, MGB HGe 4/4^{II}, MÁV V43	Now part of Stadler and Adtranz.
Softronic	Craiova	Romania	CFR Class 477	Still active; the only railway manufacturer left in SE Europe.
Sorefame (Sociedades Reunidas de Fabricações Metálicas)	Amadora, Lisbon	Portugal	CP 1200, 1400, 1900, 2500, 2601	Bought by ABB in 1997, then Adtranz, finally Bombardier; closed in 2005.
TSM	Martin	Czech Republic	ČSD Class 735	Still active.
Tülomsaş (Türkiye Lokomotif ve Motor Sanayi Anonim Şirketi)	Eskişehir.	Turkey	TCDD DE 22	Built under licence of General Electric.
TŽV Gredelj (Tvornica željezničkih vozila Gredelj d.o.o.)	Zagreb	Croatia	JŽ Class 441	Still active.

Manufacturer	City	Country	Classes of loco(s) featured	History/Notes
UCM Resita	Resita	Romania	JŽ Class 441	Still active.
Union Gießerei	Borsig	Germany	Prussian T11/DR Class 74	Became a subsidiary of F. Schichau in 1931; operating in Bremerhaven until 2009.
VEB Lokomotivbau Karl Marx Babelsberg (LKM)	Babelsberg, Potsdam	Germany	DR Class 118, 99.23, 65.10, 99.77-79	Formerly Orenstein & Koppel; bankrupt and closed in 1992.
VEB Lokomotivbau und Elektrotechnische Werke Hennigsdorf (LEW)	Hennigsdorf, Berlin	Germany	DR Class 114, 142, 143, 155, 171	Founded by AEG; returned to AEG in 1990, then Adtranz, now Bombardier.

Further reading from  KEY
Publishing

As Europe's leading transport publisher, we produce
a wide range of market-leading railway magazines.

Visit: shop.keypublishing.com for more details